Happy Holidays

Happy Holidays

Frank Minirth
Don Hawkins
Paul Meier

BAKER BOOK HOUSE
Grand Rapids, Michigan 49516

Copyright 1990 by Baker Book House Company

ISBN: 0-8010-6272-1

Third printing, February 1991

Printed in the United States of America

The authors would like to express appreciation

To
Debi Stack
for her extensive editorial work

To
Vicky Warren,
Irene Swindell
and **Kathy Short**
for manuscript typing and revisions.

Contents

For further information regarding
the nationwide services of the
Minirth-Meier Clinic, please call

1-800-545-1819

1

How Happy Are the Holidays?

What is the happiest time of the year?

Many would immediately respond to that question, "The holidays," usually meaning that time of year from Thanksgiving through Christmas to New Year's Day. The phrase "Happy Holidays," is sung, seen frequently on greeting cards, and used as a background for media advertising around the end of each year, reflecting the commonly held notion that holidays are always happy times. The familiar images appear—families opening presents and smiling over what they have received, groups gathering with delight around elaborately decorated Christmas trees and heavily laden dining room tables or joyfully singing Yuletide carols.

Years of experience in counseling have demonstrated to us that "holidays" (in the broad sense of the term) are not always happy occasions. Whether it be the Christmas or Easter season, or secular festivals such as the Fourth of July, birthdays, anniversaries, and the like, holidays can be depressing and stress-producing times for many individuals who are relatively "healthy" and full-functioning the rest of the year. To avoid any possible confusion in terms, we define *stress* as the effect, real or perceived, of circumstances or external factors or forces in our lives. Perception is a key factor. *Depression* is debilitating sadness due to anger turned inward, often resulting from the effects of stress.

When the counselor guided Ann into his office, he thought, *How surprising to see someone so grim and tight-lipped the week before Christmas.* As the counseling session began, it became obvious that a bout of holiday blues was something with which Ann was quite experienced. The counselor learned that Ann, in her mid-thirties and a wife and mother of three, frequently felt it necessary to see a counselor during the time leading up to Christmas and other holidays. Furthermore, even the time immediately following special days was stressful for her. Ann shared with the counselor how the last few days had been marked by her explosive emotional outbursts. She asserted, "My children no longer seem to know what to expect from a mother who ignores them one day and does little or nothing to take care of household responsibilities, and then the next day, during a burst of frantic activity, blows her stack over what seems to them to be a very minor rule infraction."

After learning of Ann's intense episodes of anger (both a cause and symptom of *some* depression), the counselor asked her to relate experiences about her own childhood. Ann explained that during her first twelve years she was in poor health, which contributed to her general feelings of inadequacy and low self-esteem. As the oldest daughter, Ann felt accepted by her mother only when she performed according to parental standards. She still believes that she was always given more work than she could handle. The tasks she did manage to accomplish never seemed to be done well enough.

In fact, Ann didn't really feel "worthwhile" (accepted by her mother) until she began to be successful in extracurricular school activities as a teenager. At one point in the session, Ann blurted out, "My mother only seemed to love me when I did exactly what she wanted me to do. When I didn't, I felt that she rejected me." When asked if there were particular times when she felt most "rejected," Ann replied, "Yes, around the holidays. For Christmas and Thanksgiving, my mother was involved in all kinds of things for other people. She was active in church and had all the relatives over. She drove us kids like slaves to help keep the house clean and bake all kinds of cakes and other goodies. Holidays were just miserable then—and they still are!"

Ann's case of holiday depression is neither isolated nor unusual. At the Minirth-Meier Clinic, we have treated approximately ten thousand patients. About 75 percent of them come because of depression. Approximately 90 percent of those patients are more depressed or overstressed at holidays, particularly Christmas, than at any other time. The examples of real-life individuals such as "Ann" are representative of genuine counseling experiences, although names and certain other details have been modified.

We will attempt to search out the causes of holiday stress, unhappiness, and depression and then suggest some practical ways to help make these special times an occasion for joyful anticipation, rather than the dreaded ordeal they seem to be for so many people. As we shall see in the next chapter, happiness is one of the reasons why God established the idea of holidays.

The Bible, in both the Old and New Testaments, gives specific principles that can enable us to achieve happiness, whether at the holidays or at other times of the year. In the Old Testament, the word *ashere* is one of two

Hebrew verbs often translated "to bless." According to the *Theological Wordbook of the Old Testament*, to "be blessed," a person has to do something. Usually, this is something positive. Blessed people, for example, keep God's statutes and trust in God without equivocation (Ps. 119:1–2; Prov. 2:12; 16:20). They place themselves under the authority of God's revelation, his Torah, or Word (Ps. 31:1; cf. John 1:8–9). Note the negative warnings of Psalm 1:1—"Blessed is the man who does not walk in the counsel of the wicked or stand in the way of sinners . . . ." The same source states that the word *ashere* is used forty–four times in the Old Testament, twenty–six of which are in the Psalms and eight of which are in Proverbs. Even a cursory examination of the passages in which this word is used demonstrates the accuracy of our fundamental thesis: Happiness is the result of making appropriate choices.

The same concept can be seen in the New Testament. Here the Greek word *makarios*, which parallels the Old Testament term *ashere*, carries the significance of "to be happy." For example, Jesus tells his disciples (John 13:17), "Now that you know these things, you will be blessed if you do them." The apostle Paul writes in Romans 14:22b: "Happy is he who does not condemn himself . . ." (NASB). In each of the other New Testament references using *makarios*, happiness can be seen as a direct consequence of following God's prescription for living (Acts 26:2; 1 Cor. 7:40; 1 Peter 3:14; 4:14). The two references from 1 Peter are particularly significant because they demonstrate that an appropriate response, even to adversity and suffering, can lead to happiness.

If this is the case, why do so many people with the best of motives experience unhappiness during the holidays? Humanly speaking, none of us is perfect. We are all born of sinful parents into a sinful universe and fall short of God's ideal. Our inherited sin nature gives us a capacity to make wrong choices. Apart from the redemptive grace of Jesus Christ, we would never be able to experience genuine, lasting happiness. Current worldly tensions and circumstances of the past contribute to our spiritual unrest, particularly at holidays, when there seems to be so much to do and so many positive emotional "requirements."

Frequently, the causes of holiday negativism or apathy are deeply embedded in childhood and early environmental experiences. This was the case with Gerald, who told one of our therapists that he dreaded Christmas and, for that matter, *any* holiday, because he always became depressed. Gerald, in his mid-twenties, was a successful, career-oriented individual. His family background included a passive father and a domineering mother. Like Ann, Gerald said his mother became especially bossy and demanding around the holidays when he was a child. Even though he recalled that he felt driven to work harder and harder on household chores, Gerald expressed how little he felt he accomplished. His mother frequently reminded him of how much money was spent on his Christmas gifts and waxed eloquent regarding his unworthiness to receive them. As the oldest son, Gerald felt he bore the brunt of most family conflicts.

During one counseling session, Gerald shared that his wife was just as domineering as his mother had been. The cycle of conflict that had been present in his early childhood continued in his own home at Christmas and other holidays. Gerald admitted that he often went to the office during holidays to escape his wife's demands at home, even though he felt in a bind, whatever he did. His wife nagged him about working on the holidays, but also plagued him with household chores when he attempted to spend holidays with the family. For Gerald, there was simply no such thing as a happy holiday.

Negative parental attitudes similarly influenced the way Leslie viewed the holidays. Leslie was a sharp young career woman in her early twenties. She reported suffering from "holiday blues" and intensified bouts with premenstrual syndrome (PMS). Her counselor learned that Leslie's father was a strict disciplinarian and was also a workaholic. His critical attitude continually gave "not good enough" messages to Leslie. Her mother, who was "very moody," and grandmother apparently had both suffered periodically from severe depression. Leslie told her counselor that her mother would often use "the silent treatment" on her, especially during the holidays. When family and friends were around, there seemed to be plenty of cheer and mirth. Yet, when just Leslie and her mother and/or the immediate family were present, her mother would often completely ignore her.

Leslie also felt that holidays, especially Christmas, were frequently spoiled by her mother's constant worrying about money. Even though the family was relatively well off and even owned a vacation home, Leslie's mother was a chronic worrier who seemed to relish talking about how little money they had for Christmas, trips, or even the necessities of life.

The primary factors in some holiday depression are purely financial. At other times, unresolved interpersonal relationships are involved. Sometimes a particular holiday may serve as a bittersweet reminder of happy, never-to-be-recaptured past times, as when a loved spouse or other family member is no longer around to share in the festivities. On other occasions, we may not know, at least immediately, what the basic problem is. For example, when one distraught woman called the emergency telephone number at our counseling clinic during a holiday weekend, she asked, "Where can I get help for my mother? She's always been a strong, godly mother. Occasionally she has seemed a bit down, but last night she tried to take her life and almost succeeded. Why would someone who has always seemed able to handle the stresses of life try, almost without warning, to kill herself? Especially, why would she try to do it during this holiday?"

Happy holidays? Maybe for some. For others, these days are marked with sadness, inadequacy, exaggerated stress, anxiety, overriding depression, or even suicidal impulses.

2

Are Holidays Necessary?

Why bother with holidays if they can lead to unhappiness? Perhaps the best approach *would* be to do away with them. The important point to remember is that holidays, in and of themselves, are not the source of depression and unrest.

A biblical perspective on holidays portrays certain festivals as established by our all-knowing and all-good Creator. In fact, God came up with the idea of holidays, and he did so with several important and valid purposes in mind.

Holidays Mark Time

Probably the very first holiday for Israel was established, according to the Book of Exodus, during the time when God delivered the Israelites from the land of Egypt. After Pharaoh had repeatedly refused Moses' requests to allow the Israelites to depart, God gave clear and final instructions for the establishment of what has come to be called the Passover (Exod. 12:11). Furthermore, God said this was to take place in the first month of the new year, according to the Israelites' religious calendar (Exod. 12:2). (Israel's agricultural, or civil, calendar began in the fall and existed side by side with the religious calendar until after the exile. Today, Judaism uses the civil calendar, which has the New Year observed in the fall.) The next nine verses carefully detail a ceremony in which each household was to sacrifice a lamb, cook the lamb's flesh, and apply the lamb's blood to the upper and side posts of the door of the house in which they lived (vv. 3–11). God further explains: "This is a day you are to commemorate; for the generations to come you shall celebrate it as a festival to the LORD—a lasting ordinance" (v. 14).

A key observation is in order here: God was concerned with how the Israelites *marked time*. The Canaanite designation for the first religious month, *Abib*, literally means "fresh young ears of corn." After the captivity, the Babylonian name, *Nisan,* meaning "early" or "to start" was used (see Neh. 2:1; Esther 3:7).

Holidays and Remembering

The purpose of Passover and other holidays is appropriately designated by the word translated "memorial" (Exod. 12:14, KJV). Here, the Hebrew word *zecharone* is an object or act which brings something else to mind or which represents something else. It is based on the root word for "remember."

The concept of "remembering," according to the meaning of the root verb in Hebrew, includes both inward mental acts (such as recalling or paying attention to) and appropriate external acts (such as verbalizing, reciting, or rehearsing to others, which in turn reinforce internal remembering). In fact, the second concept lies closest to the significance of the Hebrew word (Harris, et al., *Theological Wordbook of the Old Testament*, 1:551

[Chicago: Moody, 1980]). Thus, "to remember" is "to call to mind," in contrast with forgetting or ignoring (Ps. 74:22, 23). Psalm 103 strongly encourages God's purpose that we verbally praise him and "forget not all his benefits" (v. 2). Holidays throughout Scripture are specifically designated as times to *remember*, just as Israel on the Passover was to clearly call to mind and never forget how dramatically and graciously God had delivered them from Egypt.

Each of our religious and secular holidays has a significant element of memorializing or remembrance. This is true of Easter, when we remember Christ's resurrection; and of Christmas, when we remember his birth. On Thanksgiving, we remember specific blessings associated with the founding of a colony by the Pilgrim Fathers. On the Fourth of July, we recall the freedoms on which the United States of America was built and the Declaration of Independence, which delineates certain freedoms. On Memorial Day we commemorate those who have given their lives to preserve those freedoms. On Labor Day we are reminded of those who pursued the rights of workers. These and other holidays should be occasions for both remembering and acknowledging praise to God.

Holidays and Celebrating

Another reminder from Exodus 12:14 is that certain days were to be festivals—days of feasting and celebration to the Lord. God is certainly not against appropriate celebrating or having fun. In fact, the Israelites were given a national pattern of festivals, or "sacred assemblies," in Leviticus 23. This series of annual feasts frequently involved travel to Jerusalem. For example, during the Feast of Tabernacles in that city, God not only instructed the people to camp out, or live in tentlike booths, for seven days, but to "rejoice before the LORD your God" (vv. 40–42).

Sadly, some of the festival times we enjoy today, but which originated for religious purposes, have become extremely pagan in their focus. Much of what is currently associated with the beginning of Lent (Carnival, or Mardi Gras) in certain areas of the world involves immoral activities, clearly in contrast with God's intent. We must choose biblically appropriate ways to celebrate and enjoy our holidays and recognize that depression and other emotional problems can result when we celebrate unwisely. Many counseling professionals have observed a direct correlation between alcohol abuse and "inappropriate" holiday celebration.

Worship, whether on Sunday or on special occasions, is something many of us don't fully understand. Worship is not simply going to a church or synagogue, singing hymns, or engaging in a ritualistic ceremony. Rather, the concept of worship involves giving God the praise he deserves, a thankful recognition of his magnificence. It can include a symbolic act of sacrifice and dedication, as in the Israelites' Passover celebration (Exod. 12:3–8) and Abraham's presentation of his son, Isaac, to God or simply a thankful remembrance of God's greatness and our relationship with him (Ps. 95:6–7). It might involve an act of giving to God's people materially, in recognition of his love (John 21:15-16). And it can certainly involve rejoicing (Lev. 23:40).

The very word *holiday* comes from the idea of a "holy day." The Hebrew word for holy, *kadosh*, means to set apart from sin; to devote to God. The key idea is separation and consecration. Whenever we celebrate a holiday, we should recognize it as a day set apart for God's purposes. Certainly *any* holiday, religious or secular, should be a time in which we look for the spiritual significance of what we are celebrating. Enjoying the day is appropriate, but it must be done in ways that praise and glorify God.

God instructed Moses and the Israelites regarding Passover to celebrate the festival as "a lasting ordinance." This points out how important it was to God that the Israelites regularly observed this special occasion. The same idea is used in Leviticus 16:29 of Yom Kippur (the Day of Atonement), as well as of the priests' daily spiritual service at Israel's tabernacle (Exod. 27:21; 28:43; 29:9).

Israel's Holidays

Perhaps the most comprehensive chapter on holidays found in Scripture is Leviticus 23, where God details a regular calendar of holidays, beginning with the Sabbath and Passover and continuing through the Feast of Tabernacles. Every Israelite was to include each special day as an "appointment" (*moad*) with God and as an occasion to gather with other Israelites. These "sacred assemblies" included Firstfruits, Feast of Weeks (Pentecost), and Feast of Trumpets. During these days work was prohibited and Israel was to gather for worship. Special offerings associated with worship were to be given during these ceremonies (e.g., v. 19). Furthermore, God pointed out that it was appropriate for the Israelites as they prepared for these holidays to be aware of and make provision for the poor of the land (v. 22).

We discover in Leviticus 23 a contrast between the Day of Atonement, which is designated as a day of self-denial (vv. 26–32; cf. 16:1–34), and the Feast of Tabernacles, which is designated as a time of rejoicing (v. 40). Recognizing both the spiritual and emotional needs of his people, God designated one special day for national repentance and cleansing, and another for festivities and celebration. The significance for us today is that there is an appropriate time for both. There is a need for us individually and corporately to deal with the issues of sin and guilt, which build up in our lives and can frequently lead to depression. But there is also a need for the relaxation of tension and responsibility brought about as we celebrate and rejoice.

Leviticus and other Old Testament books make extensive use of the word *shebat,* a term that suggests rest. The weekly *shebat* was a holy time of rest after six days of work, a time to remember, perhaps, the Creation chronology (Gen. 2:2–3).

Holidays and Gratitude

Although Christians today are not under Mosaic Law, we can draw conclusions about holidays that are based on God's directives to ancient Israel. Psychological studies indicate that sound mental health includes remembering both the positive and negative events of the past and dealing with the emotions involved in each. It is important spiritually to remember the significant things God has accomplished on our behalf and to express gratitude for them.

For families to enjoy time together—to remind one another of past benefits and to celebrate present joys—is especially healthy. Also important is allowing time for prayer, self-examination, and supplication, whether by families, churches, or even nations.

Holidays should always reflect gratitude to God. They should provide time to enjoy being with family and other loved ones, to take a break from the routine of daily work, and to offer worship, praise, and thanksgiving. Religious holidays, such as Christmas or Easter, and secularly designated occasions—Thanksgiving, New Year's Day, and even Independence Day, Memorial Day, and Labor Day—give us the opportunity to apply these principles in our present age when they are celebrated in ways that please God.

If you struggle personally with holiday times or perhaps feel that "Happy Holidays!" sounds like a cruel attempt at humor, we hope these insights will help you to see that the problem is not rooted in the concept itself. In fact, the principles and insights to be shared in the following pages could help you to truly experience "Happy Holidays!" Although many of the principles to be related have special significance for the Christmas season, they can certainly apply to almost any designated holiday or other special day on your personal calendar.

3

Depression: Holiday and Otherwise

How common is "depression" today? The editor of one major mental health periodical says that probably 6 percent of people in the United States are depressed at any given point in time. Other studies, plus personal counseling experience, lead us to believe that the number of people feeling a moderate to significant amount of depression may be as high as 25 percent. Between twenty and forty million American people may feel generally despondent at any given time. Half of these individuals may be seriously "depressed" to the degree that they can no longer function efficiently.

Depression can be a misunderstood and overused term. It is often used by laypeople to describe a wide spectrum of behavior, ranging from a mild and temporary mood swing to ongoing and pervasive suicidal thinking or a psychotic break with reality. Although at some period in life nearly everyone experiences short-lived feelings of depression, an all-consuming bout of despair, or "clinical depression," can be a devastating illness that affects the total being—physically, emotionally, and spiritually. Since here the causative factors are sometimes not easily identifiable by the sufferer, counseling by a trained professional may be the only way to find a "cure," if not at least a remission of the symptoms. In milder cases, the victims may be able to help themselves to some degree.

Some people never seem to feel depressed or even downhearted. A good friend of one of the authors, who was a church elder and construction supervisor, never seemed to be in anything but good spirits. He often expressed difficulty in understanding why other people "let themselves become depressed." This individual simply did not have a problem in this area. He had occasional troubles, as we all do, but worked on handling his feelings about them, and he had supportive friends with whom he verbalized his emotions and talked through solutions. Another good friend of the same author, also an elder in the church, suffered frequent bouts of despondency. This man, who experienced a great deal of stress in his professional life, tended to internalize his feelings and also struggled with conflicts left over from childhood. Both of these men were sincerely committed to God and genuinely loved their fellowman, yet one often experienced depression and the other managed to cope with whatever setbacks he encountered.

Contrary to what some sincere but overly zealous Christians might say, depression is not necessarily a sign of sin or of being out of fellowship with God. Some people have the idea that a "good Christian" should never be downhearted and that prayer and a few Bible verses can remove all depression. As counselors, we firmly believe in prayer (Eph. 6:18) and in the inerrancy of Scripture and its power to transform lives (Heb. 4:12). However, telling a depressed person to "take two Bible verses and call me in the morning" is unfairly simplistic.

Dr. Meier's booklet *Meditating for Success* states that "daily meditation on Scripture (with personal application) is the most effective means of obtaining personal joy, peace and emotional maturity." We endorse that general approach. However, not all depression can be linked to some specific sin the individual has committed or even be indicative of an impoverished faith life. In a sense, depression can be traced to the sinful condition into which the whole human race has fallen. Sin *has* made our universe imperfect, so there are times when we suffer loss or disappointment and turn our emotions inward rather than seeking solutions under God's guidance.

Characteristics of Depression

One of the simplest definitions of depression describes it as a state in which anger or other emotions are denied and/or internalized. There can be a genetic predisposition toward depression, and there are often physical complications. Happiness *is* a choice (as we explain in detail in our book of the same title). Yet, enough repressed anger has surfaced in our clients' counseling sessions to show us that pent-up hostility is the root cause of nearly all clinical depression.

The common symptoms of "holiday depression" are those that characterize depression in general. For example, a depressed person will usually demonstrate a sad countenance, whatever the circumstances, even during holidays, times when everyone seems expected to wear a smile. We have learned that, indeed, depression can often be heard in the voice or seen in the face. The sad facial expression may or may not include tears, but a depressed person's eyes may be cast down and sorrow-

ful. He or she appears discouraged, dejected, weary.
Even if one tries to hide depression by smiling, the
depression shows through.

"Painful thinking" is another characteristic of depression. For example, instead of having their spirits lifted
by an approaching holiday, thoughts of associated festivities produce only pain for depressed individuals. One
homemaker listed nineteen observations about the
upcoming Christmas season. Although seventeen were
positive, she spent the next forty-five minutes intensely
discussing the two *negative* aspects of the approaching
holiday.

Depressed individuals are consumed with painful
thoughts because they tend to become extremely intro-
spective in a self-derogatory way. They concentrate a
great deal on past mistakes, perhaps assuming blame for
earlier unhappy holiday experiences. They often feel
"guilty" even when innocent, blaming themselves for
less-than-perfect celebrations, though they were in no
way responsible. A depressed individual feels at fault for
a wide variety of real and imaginary failures and worries
excessively over all kinds of past shortcomings.

Along with this self-punishing "blues" comes a feeling
of exaggerated pessimism and hopelessness. Studies
show that about 75 percent of those who are clinically
depressed feel they will never recover. Yet, though
depressed individuals crave reassurance and affection
from others, the negative emotions they are turning
inward are also indirectly creating a deep-seated hostility toward others and/or a feeling of unworthiness about
themselves, either of which short-circuits fulfillment of
that desire. Depressed individuals are preoccupied with
themselves. Such egocentricity affects attention, concen-
tration, memory, and reasoning. Since the past is a dark
cloud and the future seems gloomy, it is no wonder that

a depressed person feels listless and is adversely affected by a low energy level and sense of futility.

Physical symptoms often accompany depression, and one of the most common is broken sleep or early awakening. Many depressed individuals fall asleep fairly easily at night, only to awaken during the late-night or early-morning hours and then have difficulty going back to sleep. Paradoxically, rather than losing sleep, other depressed people sleep too much! Appetite is also often affected, causing depressed persons to eat too much or too little. Thus, they may experience significant weight gain or weight loss. The large quantities of rich food associated with holidays can contribute to the physical gastrointestinal disturbances often experienced by those suffering from depression.

Ironically, many depressed individuals say they would prefer to have a physical illness. This may be to save face for those who feel it a sign of weakness to admit to having psychological conflicts. Or it may be a futile attempt to discover an organic—and thus curable—problem, one that might be easily treated by the miracles of modern medicine. A classic example of this are those who claim to have hypoglycemia, a condition marked by low blood sugar and determined by a six-hour glucose-tolerance test. Out of over a hundred patients who came to the Minirth-Meier Clinic thinking that hypoglycemia might explain their symptoms, only one actually had low blood sugar, and that individual's condition was borderline.

Depression is frequently accompanied by attacks of anxiety and/or agitation. A rapid heartbeat or heart palpitations may occur periodically at any time. Or, as a holiday approaches and the pace of activity picks up, depressed individuals may become more irritable. Then, since people rarely like to admit to feeling angry, especially if they are conscientious Christians, they may even more strongly deny or repress the anger. Refusing to look at negative emotions or motives is the essence of what creates anxiety, so the physical symptoms may likewise accelerate in frequency and degree around the holiday season.

Sometimes this anxiety manifests itself in full-blown panic. There may be episodes of agoraphobia—in which one fears being in large spaces, crowded areas, or any place outside of home or other safe havens. Such panic attacks can be particularly severe during the frantic rush of crowded holiday celebrations or shopping trips. More commonly, anxiety can distract an individual from the activities and relationships that might normally characterize the celebration of a holiday.

Another major symptom of depression (which occasionally surfaces only during the holidays) is "delusional thinking," which differs from "painful thinking" only in degree. The delusional thinkers actually lose touch with reality. Their delusions may involve notions of persecution (they think everyone is out to get them) or grandiose assumptions (they think God has given them some special gift or insight). Individuals so afflicted may hear voices that no one else hears or see things that no one else sees. Although this usually occurs only in severe and persistent clinical depression, it is possible for an individual to experience delusional thinking during short periods of intense stress.

When individuals are undergoing such intense depressive pain that a break with reality has occurred, it is imperative to provide proper medical and psychiatric care as quickly as possible. Individuals treated soon after the delusions are first experienced can usually be restored to normality and will eventually be able to think clearly and lead fulfilling lives. Certain medications are frequently used to restore the chemical imbalances in the brain that can lead to delusional thinking. Generally, one or two months of hospitalization might be needed—with daily psychotherapy, antipsychotic and antidepressant medications, and personal support and encouragement included in the treatment program. A permanent psychotic state could be the tragic result for those whose symptoms are not recognized early enough and for whom proper care is not afforded.

Causes of Depression

Many specific factors are involved in triggering depression, but most of them bear some reference to our *expectations.* We live in an imperfect world as imperfect people. Since we are "only human," we tend to expect certain things from circumstances and other people. Since expectations frequently center on special occasions, unfulfillment of holiday hopes can certainly lead to seasonal depression. Proverbs 13:12 states, "Hope deferred makes the heart sick, but a longing fulfilled is a tree of life." This accurately explains why unfulfilled expectations can leave one heart-weary and disappointed at any time of the year. (See chapter 5.)

Closely related to our expectations is the loss component. Depression is often connected with what we call a grief reaction, brought on by a real or perceived loss. Some years ago, a special research project was developed to measure the relative effects of major life stresses on an individual. The greatest source of personal stress and the greatest sense of loss come from the death of a mate. This is followed closely in intensity by divorce. Other stress factors cited include the death of other loved ones, one's own health crises, change in a job, relocation, and so on. Each of these situations involves some sort of "loss" of status quo and, depending on the circumstances, brings disappointment or grief in the past and uncertainty about the future. In fact, it would not be inaccurate to say that "the grieving process is what depression is all about."

Our book *Happiness Is a Choice* lists five stages of grief:

1. Denial—refusing to believe the loss is really happening.
2. Anger—feeling anger toward the person who died, toward caregivers, or even toward God for allowing the loss to occur.
3. Guilt—turning anger inward, feeling remorse for the anger toward God and the others that occurred in stage two.
4. Genuine grief—having a good cry, which is very important in accepting the reality of a significant loss or reversal.
5. Resolution—regaining joy and zest for life.

A more detailed description of the mechanics and stages of grief will be found in chapter 10. For our purposes here, suffice it to be said that many episodes of depression can be traced to a failure to resolve each of these stages. Serious emotional problems can develop if the process is short-circuited or if an individual becomes fixated at one stage and never moves to the next. It is in such cases that professional counseling may be needed to help the person move on and get beyond the tragic situation.

We usually have no problem understanding our own grief reaction in severe cases, such as occurs after loss of a spouse or other family member, divorce, or other major affliction. However, the world in which we live is not always so tolerant of our reactions to loss of disappointment, whatever its nature. Often, well-meaning but naive individuals tell us, "Don't worry about losing your job. Other opportunities will come your way," or "Snap out of it! You need to handle the bad along with the good." Such misguided pat answers overlook the essential need for us to deal with our setbacks and distress (big or little, real or imagined) in a constructive manner if we are to avoid becoming depressed to the point of malfunctioning.

4

The Deception
of Idealized Memories

A colleague of ours, Dr. Chris Thurman, recently wrote a book titled *The Lies We Believe*. Most people who pick up his book and simply glance at the title are tempted to react, "Who, me? I'm a realist. I can spot the truth behind the fancy wrappings!" But, as Dr. Thurman points out (not only in his book but also in the group therapy sessions he conducts at our hospital unit), all of us occasionally engage in faulty thinking by allowing ourselves to believe certain lies—myths or exaggerated versions of reality. Wishful thinking or other emotional factors can cause us to idealize our memories of holidays and trigger holiday depression if these distorted perceptions are not reflected in present-day reality.

Selective Attention

One of the most common flaws in thinking is "selective attention," wherein we focus exclusively on either the good or the bad. When it comes to holidays, we often tend to idealize "the good old days" of our youth.

For example, one of the authors finds it easy to remember delicious turkey dinners with cornbread dressing and giblet gravy. He recalls gatherings of parents, aunts, uncles, and cousins, all dressed up and happily exchanging gifts at Christmas. He admits that seldom does he focus on family quarrels, irritating scraps with cousins, sarcastic aunts, or alcoholic uncles—though they no doubt were sometimes part of the scenario.

This man is not alone in practicing selective attention. We all tend to repress, or eliminate from conscious memory, the bad things that happen. Remembering happy times is easier and much less painful than recalling embarrassing episodes and acute disappointments. For most people, an alcoholic father or no gift under the Christmas tree is not exactly greeting-card material. Selective attention allows us to "edit out" negative holiday memories and dwell instead on the times when carols were joyfully sung and we received everything on our Christmas list. Such idealization of the past offers stiff competition for the present holidays.

To see how this works, try writing down a list of fifty things that happened during your early childhood years. Focus especially on memories associated with holidays. When you finish, go back over the list and see how many of those memories were positive and how many were negative.

More than likely, you remembered the desserts, and forgot the hyperactivity of the kids pinging off the walls because of eating too many sweets. You may have remembered the excitement of opening presents, but forgot that sick feeling in the pit of your stomach when you came to the last package, opened it, and asked yourself, "Is that all there is?" You probably also forgot about your parents' arguments over how expensive Christmas was, and how they couldn't afford the G.I. Joe kit with ten action figures. You may not recall becoming bored after playing only half an hour with the new toys. Perhaps you omitted from the list your mother's irritation when she had to clean up alone. Maybe you overlooked your dad's anger when he saw the electric trains, which took hours for him to assemble, abandoned after a few moments of play.

Sometimes, of course, selective attention *does* focus on the negative, as happened in at least one biblical narrative. This obvious case can be seen in the people of Israel who, when traveling from Egypt to the Promised Land, quickly tired of and complained about the manna that God had provided for them to eat rather than giving thanks for their deliverance from oppression. Numbers 11:4–6 reads:

> The rabble with them began to crave other food, and again the Israelites started wailing and said, "If only we had meat to eat! We remember the fish we ate in Egypt at no cost—also the cucumbers, melons, leeks, onions and garlic. But now we have lost our appetite; we never see anything but this manna!"

Verse 20 concludes, "Why did we ever leave Egypt?"

Before we judge the Israelites too harshly, let's imagine being in that situation ourselves. Anyone who enjoys eating knows how important variety is. Food is designed by God to please our senses through color, aroma, texture, and flavor. A little understanding of manna explains why the Israelites were so quick to become dissatisfied with this unusual though nourishing food.

The Hebrew word, pronounced *man-'hu* by the Israelites, literally means, "What is it?" Manna was certainly unique and not something that (as far as we know) could be identified with any of the basic food groups. Apparently, the thin flakes of manna were neutral white in color like the coriander seed, an herb with which the Israelites were familiar (Exod. 16:14; Num. 11:7–9). Since manna had a consistency like resin, it was probably a little sticky. It probably also tasted rather bland. This light-colored food, perhaps similar to honey wafers, is said to have "tasted like something made with olive oil" (Num. 11:8). And though we today have Hamburger Helper to disguise commonplace food, the Israelites had no "Manna Helper" available. No wonder they weren't jumping up and down with ecstasy over this food!

Slanted Comparison

Selective attention usually involves "slanted comparison," in which we recall the past as greatly superior to the present—often without regard to accuracy. A paraphrase of 1 Corinthians 10:12b could read, "Those who compare one time with another are not wise." Ecclesiastes 7:10 warns, "Do not say, 'Why were the former days better than these?' For it is not wise to ask such questions." Selective attention (which causes us to idealize past memories) plus its corollary, slanted comparison, can easily lead to holiday depression.

In Psalm 89:49, Ethan the Ezrahite laments God's discipline of Israel following the days of David. He writes, "O LORD, where is your former great love, which in your faithfulness you swore to David?" Undoubtedly, many in Israel, especially during festive holiday occasions in the centuries following David and Solomon, looked back on those golden years and selectively focused on God's blessing of the past. The attitude expressed by Ethan will one day be answered gloriously in the context of the millennium, as God promises through Isaiah: " . . . the past troubles will be forgotten and hidden from my eyes.

Behold I will create new heavens and a new earth . . ."
(Isa. 65:16-17).

However, we are not yet living in the time of millen-
nial blessing. Ours is a fallen era in which we engage in
defense mechanisms that are simply ways in which we
deceive ourselves about the truth to avoid facing what is
painful.

Flawed Identification

Closely associated with idealizing past memories is an
unrealistic phenomenon we call identification. Some
years ago, a television network presented "The Home-
coming," a moving story of a family that faced adversity
with courage and faith during the Christmas holidays.
This made-for-television movie led to the long-running
series, "The Waltons." Although this and similar holiday
specials are among the least offensive programs presented, they tend to instill a sense of "everybody's happy
during the holidays," which simply is not accurate.

Advertising techniques and symbols are partly responsible for producing flawed or false identification.
Through the marvels of media hype, all kinds of problems can be solved in sixty seconds or less. Stresses and
conflicts can be banished in the twinkling of an eye as
we switch to scenes of happy family members and
friends exchanging presents, shopping, partying, and
enjoying holidays with one another in glorified ways
that are seldom really experienced.

Janice, for example, was a college freshman who
could not remember a bad Christmas (selective attention). Even the heart-tugging TV coffee commercial
depicting a son's arriving home from college for the
holidays could not rival the welcome Janice was antici-
pating (flawed identification setting up unrealistic
expectations).

The long trip home seemed short as Janice recalled the many wonderful Christmases she had enjoyed in the past (idealization of memories). The task of selecting the Christmas tree had always belonged to Janice and her father (she chose not to remember the times they fussed over price and size and that he was not always so willing to participate). Cookie baking was a joint project for Mother and Janice's siblings (Mother sometimes complained and the kids argued incessantly). In her memory, the night to decorate the tree was almost a holiday in itself (even then there was lots of bickering). On Christmas Eve, the family would take a drive to admire the Christmas lights (with Dad complaining about the traffic).

Poor Janice was setting herself up for an inevitable letdown. Not only were her memories of past holidays incomplete and distorted, but she had forgotten that circumstances were bound to change the way things would be this year. One change would be the size of the family circle. Her two older siblings now had families of their own and were prevented by distance and financial considerations from making the trip "back home." Janice's younger brother still lived at home and was now a popular teenager. He made it plain that he preferred attending certain high school events to staying around home with what remained of the family.

Meanwhile, Dad had recently been temporarily laid off at work and was struggling with the bills from Mom's surgery that fall. There *was* a Christmas tree, but Dad had gone alone to purchase it before Janice's arrival, and it was too small to accommodate many of the ornaments used in the past. Fortunately Mom was now feeling much better, though not quite up to holiday baking. Since not much shopping had been done, there were few presents to wrap as a family, another "tradition" now eliminated. To top it all off, the mayor and council had successfully urged the citizenry to "conserve energy" by reducing the usual sparkling array of lighting around town.

Sure, there was a holiday turkey (smaller than usual) and an adequate sampling of go-alongs. There was the tiny tree glittering on the corner table and scattered gifts from faraway loved ones. But somehow the house was so quiet—everything seemed empty and meaningless to Janice. This was hardly the Christmas she had imagined, so she was disappointed, yet bewildered as to why she began to feel so terribly depressed, even as the depleted family circle sang the old carols in front of the fireplace.

Can you identify the dynamics here? Janice's *selective attention* and *flawed identification* (that TV commercial) brought about unrealistic expectations that, when *unfulfilled*, inevitably instilled a *slanted comparison* and *sense of loss*. The final result was sadness and *depression*.

This is only one case study, but it serves to illustrate the principle that a failure to identify reality in our memories can bring about intense disappointment. (Falling into the trap of unfulfilled expectations is the topic of chapter 5, and the unique pressures women face due to false (faulty) identification will be addressed in chapter 6.)

Facing Reality

In this chapter we have focused on three related kinds of distorted thinking that may lead to holiday depression—selective attention, slanted comparison, and flawed (false) identification. The common denominator among all three of these is self-deception. According to the prophet Jeremiah, the heart's deceitfulness is experienced by every single human being as a result of total depravity (Jer. 17:9). Modern psychology describes self-deception in terms of defense mechanisms, ways we react to frustration and conflict by fooling ourselves, thereby maintaining our self-esteem and avoiding anxiety.

Scripture presents insight about the antidote to such self-trickery and the ultimate answer for the underlying faulty thinking. The psalmist David, in confessing his sin toward Bathsheba and Uriah, recognized the importance of gaining understanding of our true motives and emotions and allowing God's wisdom to help us overcome our shortcomings: "Surely you desire truth in the inner parts; you teach me wisdom in the inmost place" (Ps. 51:6). Elsewhere in his writings, David asked God to search out his inner motives to evaluate his anxious thoughts, and to bring his heart and meditations to the point where they are pleasing to God (Ps. 19:12–14; 139:23–24).

Since self-deception and other forms of faulty thinking are as great a problem for contemporary people as they were in David's day, it is important to recognize the resources that God has provided to enlighten our minds and eliminate our blind spots. Scripture points to three such resources for Christians:

1. *The Word of God (Heb. 4:12)*. Here the author of Hebrews points out how Scripture, "sharper than any double-edged sword," can penetrate to the innermost recesses of our being and pinpoint the true nature of our thoughts and motives. The more we expose our minds and hearts to Scripture, the more likely we are to overcome our mental blocks and spiritual blindness and their debilitating or even self-destructive consequences.

2. *The Spirit of God (1 Cor. 2:10–16)*. The natural man is incapable of fully understanding and responding to spiritual truth. Yet, as Paul points out, each believer has the third person of the Trinity living within to provide insight. We utilize the Holy Spirit as a resource to the

degree that we rely on him to direct our thoughts. He can guard us from self-deceptive thinking and the other defense mechanisms we use subconsciously to "explain" why we feel as we do (as, for example, why the holiday season is one big disappointment) or to protect ourselves from dealing with the negative feelings evoked by dealing with experiences and relationships that have caused us pain.

3. *Feedback from other people (Heb. 3:13).* Daily exhortation from other believers can keep us from being hardened by a distorted view of reality and open our hearts to God's purposes. Sinful behavior often originates in self-deceptive thought patterns. Other believers may be able to warn us of perceptual errors of which we are unaware and help us see more clearly the truth about ourselves and our place in God's world, thus strengthening our protection from sin's deceitfulness.

5

The Expectation Trap

The sounds and smells of Christmas morning were everywhere. Coffee was perking and sweet rolls baking. Packages were being unwrapped as several family members laughed and called to one another excitedly. Yet, Mom and Dad looked at each other as they detected, almost at the same time, a discordant note. Sitting alone in a corner was Troy, crying his eyes out. "Son, what's wrong?" they both asked. "Don't you like your new bike?"

"But it's only a three-speed," twelve-year-old Troy replied. "I thought I was getting a ten-speed racer." Mom and Dad sighed as they exchanged meaningful glances, both realizing that Troy had fallen into the trap of unfulfilled expectations.

An examination of psychiatric or psychological studies is not necessary to discover the truth that disappointment is at the core of a great deal of human unhappiness, even misery. Most healthy people expect to be happy, satisfied, and successful—to feel significant and, perhaps to some extent, superior when those expectations are fulfilled. "Surprises" are not always happy occasions.

The Media's Seductions

Each of the five billion people on Planet Earth experiences a certain measure of inferiority. As a result, we compete with each other for attention. We are led to strive for a culturally defined and media-reinforced brand of achievement that perpetuates the myth that material gain and social success are readily attainable and will make us happy. Nevertheless, our counseling experience has shown that hundreds of people, regardless of their economic level and/or social acceptance, have experienced mental health problems and interpersonal conflicts because they were influenced to a large extent by the values communicated by the entertainment and advertising media.

We have heard words of discouragement from the lips of executives who sought to climb the corporate ladder of success like J. R. on "Dallas"; regrets from wives who felt that a mid-life affair, like those portrayed on daytime and evening soap operas, could add zest and meaning to life; and financial panic from men and women who had fallen into the trap of easy credit represented so glitteringly in TV and printed advertising. Ultimately, all were brought to a jolting confrontation with the reality that their goals were flawed. Values are indeed influenced by the media. When those values are unsound or out-of-reach they bear the potential for unhappiness.

Television seems to exert the most influence. Surveys show that the TV is on for seven hours each day in the average household. Many programs present questionable value systems to which the viewers, if exposed long enough, will tend to drift. For example, seldom are the consequences of immoral sexual behavior dealt with in situation comedies or dramas. An exception was shown a few years ago with the death of a character on "St. Elsewhere." Just before dying of AIDS, the character asserted, "We were told in our generation that love was free. And I didn't think we'd ever have to pay."

Unscrupulous business tactics, even violence, are portrayed as the route to financial coups, and interoffice situations are shown as a competitive playing field. And, though liquor is banned from on-screen advertising (except for beer and wine, for some unknown reason), an alcoholic drink is frequently hoisted by a "hero" of the small screen.

Both screened and printed commercials utilize sex appeal to sell everything from cars to dishwashing detergent. Shaving cream ads imply they will make men more virile. Fashion and cosmetics blurbs promise women more allure. By and large, we expect these promises to be fulfilled when we buy the products.

The Snare of Worldliness

Many centuries ago a wise man named John, a leader in the early church who had spent a great deal of time with Jesus and absorbed his teachings, penned some significant advice:

> Do not love the world or anything in the world. If anyone loves the world, the love of the Father is not in him. For everything in the world—the cravings of sinful man, the lust of his eyes, and the boasting of what he has and does—comes not from the Father, but from the world. The world and its desires pass away, but the man who does the will of God lives forever (1 John 2:15–17).

In these verses, John is not discussing the world created by God or the problems with the earth's ecology. Rather, he is focusing on a world *system* that is not of

God's making and thus promises to fulfill expectations through inappropriate ways: immoral thoughts and experiences ("the cravings of sinful man"); materialism, an excessive object-oriented desire ("the lust of his eyes"); and prideful struggles for prestige, personal power, or influence ("the boasting").

Many Christians have succumbed to the simplistic idea that worldliness consists of what you do or do not eat or drink, the people with whom you do or do not associate, and committing anything on a "dirty dozen" list of activities. Still, people who would never admit to being worldly are, in reality, just that.

The holidays can be one of the most susceptible times, a season when "the world and its desires" can ensnare us. For example, end-of-year office parties can lead to a relaxing of normal workplace protocol and therefore to sexual temptation. Our counseling experience has shown that many people initially fell into extramarital affairs because they drank at a party and lost their inhibitions.

"Cravings" are not limited to sex. Holidays are also times when people are tempted to overeat, going from one party to another and feasting at each gathering. Ironically, people who would never consider such a "worldly" activity as drinking alcohol succumb to the sin of overeating. Yet few Christians, even pastors, would censure an individual for gluttony. (One pastor—shortly before preaching a Sunday-evening message condemning worldliness—consumed a heaping plateful of casserole items, a bowl of salad, two pieces of layer cake, three apple turnovers, and four frosted gingerbread men at the holiday church supper.)

Another problem John mentioned is what we call materialism, which often is manifested in greed. Many people seek to prove their significance by buying everything in sight, often on credit. The incredible pressure that advertising places on us during the pre-Christmas season (which now seems to begin right after Labor Day) discourages delayed spending and focuses on immediate gratification. We are told to "just charge it." And if we possess a certain credit card, we "carry clout." Since payments on many of those pre-Christmas purchases can be delayed until February, the impulse to buy-buy-buy is further intensified. Pre-Easter, President's Day, and Thanksgiving sales add materialistic pressure to those holidays, too.

The third major problem area is referred to by John as "the boasting of what [one] has and does." This area of sin can impact the holidays, even in the church, particularly when we become involved in power struggles over where we will hold this year's choir party, who will be in charge of decorating the sanctuary, who will head up the annual children's Christmas program, or which soloist will sing "O Holy Night." We have known of cases where church splits resulted from strong-willed individuals' struggles for control of the Christmas cantata or children's pageant.

Another way this "boasting" can taint the holidays is through the inordinate pride that comes with receiving an extraordinary present and then showing it off to others. Joseph arrogantly displayed his "coat of many colors" to his brothers as a treasured gift from his father and played on their covetous envy. Perhaps more subtly, we may engage in *giving* that most impressive of gifts just to let the recipient and others know how loving and thoughtful we are!

Too many people feel that if their desires for pleasure, possessions, and prestige were not met during the year, an upcoming holiday will be their turn to have those expectations met. This type of thinking provides two roads to holiday depression: bittersweet fulfillment or the agony of unfulfilled longings.

Redefining "Contentment"

Focusing on unfulfilled expectations is usually the result of a general lack of contentment in everyday life. This is frequently a missing ingredient in our society, which lives by the motto, "You only go around once in life, so grab all the gusto you can." While there is a place for a positive "go for it" mentality, immorality and materialism and pride are not appropriate areas in which Christians should apply this concept. As a matter of fact, much of the media marketing of our day is designed to replace the idea of contentment with an obsessive desire for more and more of everything, no matter how much one already has.

In reality, contentment is foreign to human nature, at least if it is linked to externals. As he writes to express appreciation to the Philippians for a gift they had sent to him (Phil. 4:10–20), the apostle Paul indicates that although he has known what it is to be in need, God has shown him how "to be content whatever the circumstances" (v. 11). He suggests that contentment is learned through a process and even constitutes a "secret" part of the Christian faith (v. 12). Such contentment is possible because of the indwelling power of Christ (v. 13).

The concept of contentment is reflected in Paul's use of *autarkes,* a term borrowed from Epitetus and other Stoic writers. This term basically describes an individual who had learned to live independently of external circumstances. The Stoics took this concept to the extreme by regarding personal self-sufficiency as the ultimate virtue. Paul moves it to its proper biblical focus by noting that the sufficiency of Christ, not human determination, enables us to be unaffected by circumstances, "whether living in plenty or in want" (v. 12).

The apostle uses this same term in two other key passages. In the context of instructions on generous giving, Paul calls the Corinthians' attention to the sufficiency available through God's grace for every good work (2 Cor. 9:8). Writing to warn Timothy and those to whom he ministered of the dangers of loving money (1 Tim. 6:6–10), Paul shares an important formula for successful living: "godliness with contentment is great gain" (v. 6). To make sure Timothy gets the point, Paul reminds him of an important life axiom first mentioned in Job 1:21: "For we brought nothing into the world, and we can take nothing out of it" (v. 7). The implications for practical living are evident. We ought to be content with having our basic needs provided for (v. 8), needs which God has promised to meet.

Moving from this premise to the problem of unfulfilled expectations, Paul points out that those who "want to get rich" (that is, those who have strong, unfulfilled materialistic expectations) face a wide range of dangers. The apostle paints several vivid word pictures to underscore the peril faced by those whose unfulfilled desires counter contentment (vv. 9–10):

1. They are likely to be trapped by temptation.
2. They face many foolish and harmful desires.
3. They are likely to be plunged into ruin and destruction.
4. They are tested spiritually, and face the possibility of failing such tests.

Paul accurately describes people with intense material expectations—the verb he uses indicates those who grasp at material things with eagerness. Paul's point is that those who have wandered away from spiritual priorities are like individuals caught in a brier patch, having "pierced themselves with many griefs" (v. 10).

Two of the authors and several friends once took a trail ride in the hills of Arkansas. Riding horseback for miles through beautiful country, everyone enjoyed the scenery and fellowship. However, darkness fell just before the riders reached their destination. Lacking adequate light, they soon lost their way and found themselves riding through thick stands of brush, some with lengthy thorns. Obviously, the result was a great deal of misery and physical pain. This is precisely the picture painted by the apostle Paul of those who are strongly motivated by material desires.

The Distortions of Conditional Love

Discontent not only has a close tie to unfulfilled material expectations, but it can also be related to several other important concepts, one of which is a misunderstanding of what "love" is all about. Unconditional love—the kind exemplified by God—is accepting, whereas conditional love says, "I love you as long as [or *if*] you . . ." Many people would complete this definition with "as long as you provide the things I want." Whether in a parent-child relationship, a marriage, or a friendship, unconditional love and contentment go hand-in-hand. Conditional love is qualified by "fine print" stipulations and fosters the discontent we feel when others do not fulfill our expectations.

The Poison of Selfishness

Another important correlation can be seen between unfulfilled expectations and preoccupation with self. The 1980s have accurately been termed the "Me Decade." Everywhere we are called upon to "self-actualize" (whatever that means), to "do our own thing" and "look out for number one." Yet Christians recognize that servanthood is to be a guiding principle of their faith.

Scripture is full of warnings against exaggerated pride and self-preoccupation. Jesus, the Suffering Servant, told us, "If anyone wants to be first, he must be the very last, and the servant of all" (Mark 9:35). Paul warned us not to think of ourselves more highly than we ought (Rom. 12:3). Often, human selfishness is at the heart of unfulfilled expectations. Yet we frequently deny being selfish because, in a manner consistent with Jeremiah 17:9, we deceive ourselves into thinking we are something we are not.

Delores, for example, is a lonely and bitter single woman. Her self-centered attitude of "everyone else has more than I do" has left her caught in a trap of unsatisfied longings and a friendless existence. If Delores could put herself aside occasionally and dwell on how she might serve others, she would experience relief from her selfish envy and gain friends in the process. To the degree that we focus on our relationships with God and others, we will be able to experience greater contentment, even when facing unfulfilled expectations.

One of the major emphases in Scripture is on remembering *all* God's benefits to us (Ps. 103:2), the greatest being his redemptive and forgiving love. In his stirring indictment of the human race's depravity, Paul adds a seemingly innocuous and unrelated statement. Yet this simple phrase pinpoints the essence of how we are to handle our unfulfilled expectations: "For although they knew God, they neither glorified him as God nor gave thanks to him, but their thinking became futile and their foolish hearts were darkened" (Rom. 1:21).

Time after time we have counseled angry, bitter individuals who felt life had cheated them because they had expectations, many of them material, that were unfulfilled. One of our major counseling strategies is to motivate such individuals to experience, often for the first time, a spirit of thankfulness, an attitude of gratitude for whatever they *do* have.

Unfulfilled Expectations and Parenting

A final warning regarding unfulfilled expectations is appropriate here. Some parents unwittingly sow the seeds of discontent for their children by promising them the moon when it comes to holiday gift giving (which includes birthdays and graduations). This is often because the parents are convinced they must give more and do more to prove their love for a child. Or it may simply be a matter of personal pride, an effort to keep up with the Joneses or with an ex-spouse who indulges the children.

For example, if every boy in the neighborhood has the latest model Vision skateboard and your son has a five-year-old Sears-Roebuck model, you may be tempted to think that somehow you are less loving as a parent. Many of us promise our children the right skateboard, stereo, computer, or whatever, when we simply can't deliver without breaking the budget. Promising less and then overfulfilling is better than promising too much and leaving those expectations unfulfilled or following through with a foolish extravagance that teaches the child very little about the real world.

Parents also shape how their children handle unfulfilled expectations by the way in which they handle their own. We all know what imitators our children can be. Do they see you focusing so intently on a wish list of expectations (different job, new house) that you pout and become angry when they are unfulfilled? Or do they see you committing your needs and wants to God and then trusting him to provide in his own way at his own time?

Chapter 12 offers practical, nitty-gritty advice for freeing yourself and your family from the trap of self-imposed holiday expectations. Suggestions are also given for handling the unique media pressure that contributes to our setting up unrealistic, and consequently unfulfilled, expectations.

6

Holiday Burnout (and the Martha Complex)

Remember Janice, the college student in chapter 4? She came home for Christmas one year expecting a Frank Capra holiday but ended up depressed. She was too wrapped up in how she *wanted* things to be to understand the lack of Yuletide spirit, and even that her usually active mother, though partially recovered from her recent surgery, was "too tired to drag out all that stuff and deal with baking." Or that Dad was too stressed about his job situation to deal with the nostalgic chores of former holiday seasons. Janice's parents had reached their limit in dealing with the pressures of ordinary life. Adding the demands of holiday niceties was simply too much. They were burned out, and Janice was disappointed.

We hear a great deal about burnout these days. It's a term found with increasing frequency in the business world, and even in ministry. Although one of the primary purposes of holidays is to provide a relaxing and refreshing change of pace, for many individuals the holidays are times of burnout because they add, along with the joy, the pressure of extra activities and scheduling.

The Nature of Burnout

What exactly is burnout? Psychologist Christina Maslach, in her book *Burnout: The Cost of Caring*, defines it as "a syndrome composed of emotional exhaustion, depersonalization or the desire to withdraw from people, and reduced accomplishment." Like burnout on the job or in a marriage, holiday burnout reflects the general principle that humans have a stress threshold.

While men can experience holiday burnout—and some do because of financial pressure, overinvolvement in end-of-year job responsibilities, family gatherings, church functions, and long hours assembling complex toys before Christmas morning—it is probably more common for women to experience its symptoms. Again, media hype is largely responsible. (This was discussed in chapter 5 as it relates to unfulfilled expectations.) However, advertising and TV specials also perpetuate unrealistic identification. People are shown on television happily purchasing expensive Christmas gifts, not being told by a salesclerk, "I'm sorry, your credit card has been refused." The new father, who serves in the military and has never seen his baby daughter, comes home for the holidays at the last minute, providing a neat ending for yet another program, but even that joyous occasion can bring a degree of stress in real life.

And women are shown juggling a myriad of responsibilities with the patience of Job and the wardrobe of a fashionable "best dressed" nominee. From her moussed hair to her manicured fingernails, the typical TV heroine has it all together. Her leather pumps never break stride, not even when fitting holidays into an already full schedule that may combine homemaking with an out-side job.

Women, who typically are responsible for the details of holiday celebrations, are put under additional pressure by magazines whose covers boast the ultimate in entertaining. The inference is that with just a few dollars invested in purchasing this magazine, any woman holds the key to making the best Christmas [Thanksgiving, Easter, Fourth of July] that her family has ever known. What the printed matter fails to say is that the twelve-course dinner, five-tier cake, and seventy-three hand-made gifts were done weeks in advance by a paid staff of professionals! Not surprisingly, then, women who expect to copy such feats on their own become frazzled, angry, depressed—burned out.

Television and radio talk shows also share tips on creating warm holiday memories. Suggestions abound for quick-easy-inexpensive dishes, decorations, and gifts. Are such suggestions realistic? Is there a hidden message in these programs that women who do not personally design meaningful family traditions are failures? Sometimes the implication is that children will always have an inner void because their moms never dressed like Pilgrims on Thanksgiving or hand-wove their Easter baskets.

The Balance Factor

As in most areas of life, balance is the key to true success. If a woman stays up for three nights in a row to cook, clean, bake, and decorate, but is then irritable and short-tempered around her family, will her holiday efforts produce rich memories? Probably not.

No attempt is being made here to discourage women from initiating new traditions and preserving meaning-ful ones from the past. When kept in proper perspective, they can provide precious times of family togetherness. But the unnecessary holiday stress and disappointment that often lead to burnout can be avoided when the goals are realistic and the emphasis for celebration is placed on the significance of the occasion and not on all the trimmings and trappings.

Another important element in balancing holiday pressures is distributing responsibilities among the people involved. For most of us, holidays are a time of high stress because of the many tasks we think we must do without help. For readers (women in particular) who are nodding or moaning in agreement, there is hope!

The Martha Complex

Romans 15:4 says, "For everything that was written in the past was written to teach us, so that through endurance and the encouragement of the Scriptures we might have hope." Because of the classic symptoms evident in Martha's experience, we might speak of holiday burnout as the Martha Complex. We can gain insight to help us avoid burnout by examining this New Testament woman who struggled with the issue of priorities.

The kind of burnout women often experience at the holidays is perhaps best seen in Luke's account of an incident in the life of Martha, a friend in whose home Jesus and his disciples frequently visited. (According to John's Gospel, Martha was the sister of Mary and of Lazarus, whom Jesus later raised from the dead.) A highly motivated, conscientious individual, Martha placed herself under intense stress while seeking to care for the domestic needs of her family and show hospitality toward her special guests.

Luke 10 relates what happened when the Savior and his disciples were visiting with Martha and her family. We might surmise that Martha's house had become a place to which Jesus and his disciples often retired to spend holidays. At this particular time Jesus was confronted by Martha because there were important projects to be accomplished in the kitchen and Mary seemed to be ignoring her part.

Luke, the physician-writer, paints a picture of an intimate conversation taking place in one part of the house, consisting primarily of Jesus talking and Mary sitting and listening. In another part of the house, "Martha was distracted by all the preparations that had to be made" (v. 40a).

Perhaps motivated by a combination of internal pressures and the extra preparations required because of the added guests (a frequent holiday stress point), Martha finally acts on her feelings. We can only speculate on her tone of voice, but her words make her feelings clear: "Lord, don't you care that my sister has left me to do the work by myself? Tell her to help me!" (v. 40b).

In response to Martha, the Lord does not deny the importance of cooking, cleaning, baking, or decorating. Rather, he calmly chooses to attract Martha's attention away from these things to what is a priority. His call to Martha, reflected in the repetition of her personal name (v. 41), implies how much he cared about her. But although he compassionately understands her anxiety and agitation about "many things," he hastens to underscore the validity and importance of taking time to do what Mary was doing: sitting and listening (v. 42).

So many times, like Martha, we are tempted to give selective attention to the many tasks that occupy our minds and hands. We mentioned earlier the importance of keeping a balance between people and projects. A friend of ours once wrote on a 3" x 5" index card the initials PAMITP—PEOPLE ARE MORE IMPORTANT THAN PROJECTS. The motto represented by those initials is good for us to remember when trying to balance the pressures of relationships and responsibilities.

When the balance is lost, we may begin to feel as tied up in knots as Martha did. She was under a lot of pressure and expressed resentment toward her sister for failing to help her and toward Jesus for encouraging Mary to sit at his feet rather than assist with the chores.

Components of Burnout

There are three components of holiday burnout: emotional exhaustion, depersonalization, and reduced accomplishment.

Emotional Exhaustion

From our counseling experience we have discovered an obvious difference between healthy physical fatigue and *emotional* exhaustion, the first component of burnout. The individual who has just returned from a brisk, early morning walk, an extended workout with weights, or a rapid-fire game of tennis may feel physically depleted but emotionally high. In fact, brisk physical exercise actually releases endorphins, a natural body chemical that promotes positive emotional feelings.

When one feels emotional exhaustion, however, positive feelings are missing. Emotional exhaustion has been described as feeling totally wiped out. Some individuals call this feeling being "zonked," which might be described as "sitting very still with no desire to move." In addition to the physical wear and tear from her exertions in the cause of hospitality, Martha's emotional reaction to Mary (and even to the Lord) undoubtedly left her feeling emotionally drained.

Holiday seasons tend to promote both physical fatigue and emotional exhaustion. We frequently wind up spending time with people we don't know very well—or may dislike—even doing things we do not enjoy. Church members may find themselves rushing to and from choir practices, cantata rehearsals, pageant-planning meetings, and providing taxi service for children's caroling. When asked to take part in these activities, people do so in ways that place both physical and emotional strain on themselves. Church socials, family gatherings, school functions, office parties—all of these take their toll on our physical, mental, and emotional resources.

Maybe you can identify with a busy pastor and his wife who sat down during a recent pre-Christmas rush to take stock of the upcoming holiday schedule. This evaluation took place on the last evening in November. The family's conclusion was that there were only three available nights before December 25 for family shopping, rest, or relaxation.

Depersonalization

The second component of burnout, one closely related to emotional exhaustion, is the depersonalization factor. At the very time when they would expect to enjoy being with other people, victims of burnout withdraw into endless projects that leave them feeling even more burned out and isolated. This seems to be what happened with Martha. Facing a choice between spending time visiting with Jesus or working on chores, Martha chose the tasks. She not only seemed to wish to be away from the conversation, her comments seemed to indicate possible resentment that others could enjoy conversation while there was work to be done.

Obviously, since the holidays do present additional domestic tasks, there is a need for balance between letting everything go and spending all our time on checklists of "must do" activities. We need to be careful that burnout doesn't cause us to withdraw from people, especially during the holidays when shared joys and companionship are such an important part of any meaningful time of celebration.

Reduced Accomplishment

The third characteristic of burnout is somewhat ironic. We don't know that Martha was working harder and accomplishing less than usual, but her boldness in confronting Jesus to enlist Mary's aid indicates that this may have been the case. Many usually capable hostesses have found their efficiency rating reduced by burnout related to holiday activities and responsibilities.

Susie, for example, was normally an extremely efficient homemaker. Yet the year she scheduled a family reunion for Easter weekend and invited twenty out-of-town guests for Easter Sunday dinner, she began experiencing the symptoms of burnout as the weekend began. For Susie, Good Friday was anything but good due to a persistent headache, then a backache. She was extremely lethargic, in contrast to her normal high-energy level. The vacuum cleaner seemed impossibly heavy to push, she forgot several essential items on her food-shopping list, and baking pies appeared to be an insurmountable task for the woman whose culinary accomplishments were renowned in the neighborhood. Yet Susie continued to push herself, so that by Saturday she was at her wit's end. As she put it later, "The harder I pushed, the further behind I got. I didn't want to cry 'uncle,' but I finally had to enlist the help of my mother-in-law."

Causes of Burnout

Like other kinds of burnout, the burnout associated with holidays is not caused by any single factor. We usually can identify three major causes: perception of current stress, personality-related tendencies, and bitterness (unresolved anger issues).

In contrast to what the word *holiday* means, these are high-stress times. The schedule is usually packed; we stay up past normal bedtime; we neglect to eat proper foods. Travel is often involved, which adds more effort and worry. Yet stress is more than the events that happen and our physiological response to them.

Perception of Current Stress

One of the major components of stress is our cognitive interpretation of events. We frequently give ourselves messages that lead to overload: "I must have the Christmas tree up and completely decorated by the day after Thanksgiving." "It would be terrible if we did not spend equal time with her parents and mine." "Our children would feel deprived if we failed to purchase all the gifts they wanted this year; after all, last year we weren't able to spend very much."

One particular area where perception enters the picture is what we might call "post-holiday depression." Somewhat similar to the postpartum depression experienced by many mothers following the birth of their babies, post-holiday depression is that "blue" feeling of disappointment we often have after Christmas or other holidays. This may be related to the aftermath of holiday pressures (real or imaginary), to unfulfilled expectations, or to such new stress-producing misconceptions as, "Things should have gone better during the holiday, and it's my fault that they didn't."

Personality-Related Tendencies

The second major cause of burnout, often the predisposing factor in holiday depression, is related to personality type. The personality most susceptible to burnout (and holiday depression) is the perfectionistic Type A, or obsessive-compulsive. Typically, such individuals place intense demands on themselves. Holiday burnout for a Type A woman can result from her inner compulsion to keep the house absolutely clean at all times, bake an over-abundance of holiday treats, wrap Christmas packages until the tree is obscured from sight behind a mountain of gifts, and provide clever decorations for every publicly visible room in the house. Type A men are not immune from the compulsion to make a holiday super-special, though their perfectionism may be manifested in less obvious ways.

Often, these inner compulsions or intense demands upon self are because of influences from early child-hood. In many cases, the parents of perfectionists extended only conditional love toward their children at significant times. As a result, perfectionists often feel that love, even God's, must be "earned." Conditional love can be particularly evident at holidays such as Christmas, when parents may bribe their children to behave by warning them, "You'll not receive anything at Christmas unless you're a *perfect* little angel."

Although parents understand the kind of *relative* per-fectionism they're talking about in terms of appropriate behavior, children frequently interpret these messages at a far more literal level. Several members of our child-and-adolescent division report that some teenagers have come to experience a holiday depression indirectly related to trying to earn the approval of a harsh and crit-ical parent (even an absent one) or other authority fig-ure, including God.

Although the obsessive-compulsive may be the most likely to experience holiday burnout, all the major per-sonality types have particular ways of relating negatively to the holidays, which can lead to burnout. Passive-aggressive individuals may find themselves withdrawing, being chronically late and delaying others. This type of person may be internally angry over being "bushed" from holiday activities and responsibilities but expresses the anger by devices more subtle than open hostility.

The attention-seeking hysteric personality may become immersed in too many activities, parties, and festivities. Financial burnout may be experienced by such a person, if he or she tries to earn the approval of others by entertaining too much or purchasing holiday gifts and finery that are beyond the budget. On the other hand, the paranoid personality type may trigger interpersonal conflicts by being controlling, harsh, or critical of others' holiday efforts. Sociopaths may become burned out from an overdose of their characteristically self-indulgent behavior, in frantic search of holiday pleasures.

Bitterness

The most significant cause of burnout (holiday or otherwise) is bitterness resulting from unresolved anger and grudges. At holiday times, especially at Christmas, resentment and bitterness that has been present for a long time may surface. This bitterness may be toward a spouse for creating sizable debts with credit cards or toward an alcoholic family member who ruined an earlier holiday because of a drunken episode. Or it could be toward parents who shattered the ideal happy early-childhood home by divorce, or long-term verbal, physical, or sexual abuse.

Bitterness, perhaps the greatest spiritual and emotional problem faced by Christians, consists of unresolved, prolonged anger. Usually a conscious or subconscious motive for revenge is present as well. In our book *How to Beat Burnout* (Moody, 1986), we list several important causes of bitterness that are paralleled by

New Testament references. Each of these can be related to holiday burnout.

1. *Wrong motives: jealousy.* At the holidays we frequently come in contact with people in ways that promote envy or jealousy. One Christmas, Leonard, who had a moderate income from his work in a Midwest medical clinic, went home for a holiday gathering with extended family. Several of his cousins were present. One had recently obtained a high-paying promotion. Another showed pictures of his European vacation. Before long, Leonard began feeling resentful and eventually burned out over the holiday reunion.

Those feelings were intensified when Leonard became embroiled in an argument with two of his cousins over Christians who succumb to materialism. Leonard had fallen into the bitterness/burnout trap described in James 4: "What causes fights and quarrels among you? Don't they come from your desires that battle within you? . . . you ask with wrong motives, that you may spend what you get on your pleasures" (vv. 1, 3). In Acts 8, Peter described Simon the magician as being "full of bitterness and captive to sin" due to his jealousy over the supernatural abilities that God had given Peter and the other apostles—abilities that Simon coveted to further his own prestige.

2. *Wrong response to irritations: conditional love.* The primary area in which this tends to surface is in immediate-family relationships, husbands to wives and parents to children (*see* Col. 3:19, 21). Any close relationship, when stressed by the added pressures of the holidays, can become resentful in response to even minor irritating factors.

Jill told the therapist about her husband, "It seems the holidays make him even more critical. Most of the time nothing I do seems to please him anyway, but he really gets upset about the money I spend on the children at the holidays. And he criticizes me for such petty little things." When Jill's husband, Joe, became involved in counseling, the marriage therapist discovered that he was repeating a pattern learned in childhood. Accepted only when he performed according to his parents' high standards, he used conditional love as a method of relating. Both Jill and Joe experienced holiday burnout—and marital burnout as well.

3. *Wrong response to adversity.* In the book *Beating the Odds*, Frank Minirth lists a number of reasons why God allows us to experience adversity. One of those is God's loving discipline, as described in Hebrews 12. Yet adversity, meant as a learning experience, can produce a "bitter root" that "grows up to cause trouble" (v. 15).

Frequently, holidays are times in which we do experience "adversity," whether we discover that the New Year's Eve outfit we planned to wear no longer fits, the Fourth of July barbecue we were cooking goes up in smoke, or a burglar makes off with the carefully purchased Christmas presents a week before the big day. (Even a relatively minor misfortune can seem calamitous when coupled with other holiday stress.)

Dan and Anna and their three young children left early on Christmas Eve for a visit to Anna's parents in another state. After driving all day and into the night, they experienced car trouble. Instead of being with family and enjoying themselves, they were stuck in a dingy motel in a small town, their car unrepaired when the mechanic was unable to obtain parts because of the holiday. Bitterness over this adversity not only led to holiday burnout that year, but future Christmases were also tainted by the bitter memories of that event.

4. *Exaggerated strife.* Conflict can rear its head at holiday seasons perhaps more than at any other time. This can occur in families because of personality clashes or in busi-

nesses when one individual is allowed to take off for a holiday and others must work to cover the load. It can even occur in churches.

For years, Elizabeth had coordinated the children's Christmas pageant at her local church. She had always enlisted the volunteers, made costumes, written the plays, and even directed them. Her husband, a skilled carpenter, had built the sets and decorations. When Sally and Richard, a new couple in the church, volunteered to help, Elizabeth initially reacted with enthusiasm.

But soon the preparation for the Christmas event turned into guerrilla warfare that led to out-and-out strife. Elizabeth and her husband began to resent the newcomers' suggestions. They became angry and bitter toward the new couple and toward their pastor for encouraging them to participate. Eventually they quit the church because of what they viewed as an implied criticism of their own efforts. Inappropriate bitterness brought strife and holiday burnout for this couple.

5. *An unforgiving spirit.* All too frequently we resist forgiving others at an emotional level, while claiming to have "forgiven and forgotten" a real or imaginary wrongdoing. When we say we have forgiven but really have not, we harbor angry grudges. Often this bitterness boils to the surface around the holidays, leaving us depressed, irritable, and burned out without understanding why. Seeing certain individuals may recall related unpleasant memories and can lead to feelings of holiday burnout, when the underlying issue is an unacknowledged, unforgiving spirit.

Ephesians 4:25–26 makes it clear that recognizing when we become angry is appropriate ("speak truthfully," but "In your anger do not sin"). The implication is that we need to become aware of the underlying emotion and deal appropriately and openly with it. We're further encouraged to "not let the sun go down" on our anger and to put away all bitterness, rage, anger, quarreling, slander, and every form of ill will and become kind, compassionate, forgiving one another (vv. 26, 31–32).

All too often we allow our holidays to be spoiled by burnout and depression that are directly related to bitterness, which is a suppressed motive for revenge. Such an attitude is expressly forbidden in numerous biblical passages (e.g., Rom. 12:19; 1 Thess. 5:14; Lev. 19:15–18).

Cynthia could not understand why she disliked the Easter season. She always felt burned out around that time and never wanted to attend sunrise services or regular Easter worship. Every Easter she looked for excuses not to gather with her relatives or her husband's family. Instead, throwing herself into spring cleaning around the home, she withdrew from people. What was Cynthia's problem? Depression and burnout that came from an unforgiving spirit.

The Christian counselor who worked with Cynthia discovered that, as a teenager, Cynthia had been deeply distressed over the break-up of her parents' marriage on an Easter weekend. This occurred right after Cynthia had obtained a beautiful new dress for an Easter musical that she no longer wanted to participate in because she was so hurt by her parents' action. She was angry with her father and mother and even angrier with God for letting it happen. Yet, suppressing her emotions over the years, Cynthia was unaware of her bitterness. She only knew that every Easter she seemed to "burn out and feel miserable."

Handling Holiday Burnout

What can we do about holiday burnout, including the Martha Complex? We will discuss specific steps for beat-

ing burnout in a later section. Of importance here is recognizing that since burnout has many aspects, we need
to deal with it appropriately at each level.

Physically, we must periodically take time out from
the activities and responsibilities of the holiday season.
We need time away from people, time to rest, time to
relax and have fun, time for personal shopping. Above
all, we need time with God, time to meditate on
Scripture. Unless we follow the exhortation of Jesus to
his disciples to "Come with me by yourselves . . . and
get some rest" (Mark 6:31), we may simply come apart
at the seams.

On an *emotional* level, we need to examine all our
underlying feelings: anger and bitterness, loneliness,
inferiority, or insecurity. Facing those emotions honestly,
choosing to deal with them appropriately, and practicing
forgiveness "as in Christ God forgave you" (Eph. 4:32)
can help you avoid the emotional overload that leads to
holiday burnout.

Finally, *spiritual* holiday burnout often results from
not remembering to "wait on the Lord." Isaiah 40:31
provides an appropriate antidote to holiday burnout:
"But those who hope in the LORD will renew their
strength. They will soar on wings like eagles; they will
run and not grow weary, they will walk and not be
faint."

When you find your strength sapped by holiday
burnout, and depression is looming just around the corner, remember and meditate on that important principle. Those who wait on the Lord—those who stretch out
faithful hearts and hands to him—can experience
renewal of strength and energy and thereby substitute
joyful anticipation for the "holiday blues."

7

Loneliness and the Holidays

During World War II, the enemy conducted experiments to determine the most effective type of punishment for prisoners of war. Numerous torture techniques were tried, but the most effective was solitary confinement. Many of those held prisoner found it possible to withstand the presence of pain or the absence of food and basic comfort. Yet, after a few days in solitary confinement, most prisoners would break down and tell and do whatever was demanded of them. Just as individuals from whom water is withheld will hallucinate about water, prisoners in solitary confinement would hallucinate about people.

John Milton described loneliness as "the first thing which God's eye named 'not good.'" C. S. Lewis, in his book *The Problem of Pain,* talked of "loneliness that spreads out like a desert."

How does loneliness contribute to holiday depression? After all, we usually think of holidays as opportunities to be with other people—whether at a crowded

Fourth of July barbecue, a church Valentine's Day banquet, or a shared Thanksgiving meal. And most people *do* manage to be physically with others at such times.

However, being alone and loneliness are two different experiences. As Charles Durham writes in his book *When You're Feeling Lonely,* "It is possible to be lonely with others around us because our inner needs are not being met." In *Why Be Lonely?* (Baker, 1982) Dr. Les Carter defines loneliness as "a state of feeling that one is not accepted or does not belong. It implies varying degrees of emotional pain, an empty feeling, a yearning to be with someone, a restlessness."

Many Christians believe that loneliness only affects emotional or social cripples, the outcasts of life. Yet Dr. Carter—husband, father, church deacon, popular radio talk-show participant, author, and counselor who spends hours helping others with their problems—shares the following:

> I wish I could tell you that I have never had to struggle with loneliness. But that would not be truthful. Because of my humanness I have been confronted with it many times. I have known the loneliness that comes after having misunderstandings with friends and family members. I have known the loneliness which results from personal rejection. I have experienced the lonely feeling that accompanies the responsibility of having to be the bearer of bad news to people dear to me. In spite of my study and knowledge of human emotions, I will never be completely immune to the ill effects of loneliness.

If well-adjusted individuals such as Dr. Carter can admit candidly to struggling with loneliness, is it any wonder that this emotion is a major factor in holiday depression?

Christ's Loneliness

Are there examples of loneliness in Scripture? More to the point, was Jesus ever lonely? Of course. Perhaps the most graphic example is of Christ on the cross, crying out those words of emotional agony, *"Eloi, Eloi, lama sabachthani?"* (Mark 15:34). The translation of these poignant Aramaic words is vivid: "My God, my God, why have you forsaken me?"

This is the ultimate moment of loneliness. Christ, as *man*, experienced every human emotion, including the desolation he felt though fulfilling his holy Father's plan for humankind's redemption. How appropriate that Christ's suffering, so as to provide the basis for our fellowship with God and with each other, involved enduring loneliness.

There were other lonely moments in the life of Christ. Certainly he must have frequently felt misunderstood and rejected. After Jesus' extended discourse on his significance as the Bread of Life (John 6), many of his followers abandoned him. Another point of loneliness must have been in the Garden of Gethsemane. There, his three closest friends were present, but they slept through his cries of agony to the Father (Matt. 26:36–45), as he sweat "drops of blood" (Luke 22:44). The loneliness of that moment must have cut deeply and painfully.

From these incidents we can see that loneliness is not a sin, since Jesus Christ was perfect and sinless. There are some Christians who callously say, "It's a sin to be lonely because it shows that you are out of fellowship with God." There are even Christian songs that express the thought that once you have trusted Christ you will never be lonely again.

Since Scripture indicates many circumstances in which

our perfect Lord and other righteous men felt loneliness
(e.g., Ps. 102; 2 Tim. 4:16), labeling loneliness as sin is both
insensitive and inaccurate. Loneliness is a symptom, an
emotional reaction that needs to be faced and dealt with
according to its underlying basis.

Having defined loneliness and described it from
Scripture, we can easily see how loneliness can contribute to holiday depression. After all, holidays are
times when we are not supposed to feel alone. We are
expected to be with people. Even so, many of our counseling patients have described their times with other
people as occasions when loneliness is felt most acutely.

In a counseling session Natalie, a wife of many years,
tearfully told of a vacation visit with her husband to his
family reunion. As she explained it, "There were people
all around. There was laughter. Everyone seemed to be
having a good time. My husband was in his element. Yet
neither he nor anyone else seemed to notice or even care
that I was there or what I was feeling. I can't even
describe how lonely I felt or how depressed I became
afterward." Significantly, this experience took place on a
holiday—Memorial Day weekend.

Who Gets Lonely?

One recent survey revealed that one out of every four
respondents admitted to being lonely within the preced-
ing few weeks. Over 10 percent reported what they
described as "severe loneliness" during the week just
concluded. The articles on loneliness in popular magazines are most frequent in those targeted toward
women, and underscoring the fact that women, whether
married or single, admit to more loneliness than men
do. Those who have lost a mate in death report loneliness to be their most serious problem.

Others who "feel lonely" are those who have never married or are recently divorced, teenagers, the elderly, minorities, and the handicapped. According to the book by Lawrence J. Crabb and Dan B. Allender, *Encouragement: The Key to Caring* (Grand Rapids: Zondervan, 1984), anyone who focuses on encouraging others, particularly those in full-time ministry, is apt to feel "profound loneliness." Another group facing severe loneliness is composed of the one-out-of-five individuals and families in America who move during any given year. Relocation is quite stressful, and in our mobile society loneliness is a major by-product of the often corporate-triggered relocation proliferation.

Understanding Loneliness

Spiritual Roots

Looking beneath the surface, we observe a number of root causes of loneliness, beginning with a lack of fellowship with God. As St. Augustine expressed it, "Thou hast made us for Thyself, and the heart of man is restless until it finds its rest in Thee." Thus, even though loneliness is essentially a psychological problem, its roots are often spiritual in nature.

The apostle John, one of the closest to Jesus of all the disciples, began his first epistle to the church with a discussion of the essence of fellowship with God, explaining that one purpose of Christ's coming was that we might have fellowship with one another (1 John 1:3–4). Fellowship involves experiencing something meaningful in common, a bond that can dispel loneliness, for loneliness and true fellowship are like oil and water—they simply do not mix.

Consequently, the ultimate solution for loneliness involves increasing our fellowship with God. This is accomplished by two measures. The first and most fundamental involves trusting Christ as Savior or, as John would describe it, "we walk in the light" (1 John 3:21). In the preface to his Gospel, John speaks of Christ as "the true light" who, coming into the world, lights every man (John 1:7). He explains that those who receive him are given the authority to become children of God, members of God's family (v. 12). This is accomplished by placing our personal faith in Jesus, God's Son, who came into this world to take away our sins by dying on the cross and who rose again from the dead to seal the promise of eternal life.

Yet, many who have trusted Christ still experience a high degree of spiritually related loneliness. Again, it is John who provides an explanation. Those who "walk in the darkness . . . do not live by the truth" (1 John 1:6). When Christians sin, there is a sense of isolation from God, and marital or family conflict can lead to similar feelings.

What is the solution? John describes the second element of maintaining fellowship with God as confessing our sins (1 John 1:9). But this does not simply mean to say, "God, I'm sorry," even if it includes a promise to "never do it again."

The Greek word for confess, *homolegeo*, means to "say the same thing." Thus, when I confess sin, I call it what it is—sin! I specifically name the sin. "God, I lied about that issue." "God, I succumbed to that lustful temptation." "God, I harbored feelings of bitterness toward you." Since God, through Christ's death, has provided complete forgiveness for every sin a believer commits, confession applies that forgiveness to our daily experience, restoring us to a position of fellowship.

Lack of Love

Essential to this discussion of fellowship and loneliness is an understanding of love. John describes love as the essence of what God is (1 John 4:8). Love originates from God. John adds, "We love because he [God] first loved us" (v. 19).

God loves us perfectly and unconditionally. Though he hates sin, he loves sinners. Of significant note is Jesus' description of our major lifetime responsibilities as involving loving relationships. When asked to name the greatest commandment, he replied, "Love the Lord your God with all your heart . . ." (Mark 12:30). The second great commandment is to love your neighbor as yourself (v. 31). So, we see that a major cause of loneliness involves a lack of love.

Love is both the glue that holds relationships together and the insulation that wards off feelings of loneliness. Since there is never a lack of love from God, the problem in that area involves either being out of fellowship with him or an actual or perceived lack of human love. In contrast to God who simply *is* love, we humans are imperfect, both in perceiving and accepting the love extended to us and in extending love to others.

Unfortunately, love is frequently missing, deficient, or unexpressed in human actions. A husband may *tell* his wife, "Honey, I love you intensely," then counter his words by investing so many hours in workaholic pursuits that he seldom spends time with her. A parent may say, "Son [or daughter], I really love you," yet constantly criticize, scold, or put down the child. Friends may profess love for us, then snub us or gossip about us when we are not around. People at church may claim to love us and even greet us warmly at the services, yet constantly pass up opportunities for close personal fellowship. All of these messages are interpreted as a lack of love, which leads to loneliness.

Loneliness from Within

Sometimes love is actually being extended, but an individual does not perceive it as such or cannot accept it. The effect is the same—a lonely feeling. Therefore, a third cause of loneliness comes from within. It mainly involves a lack of confidence, or personal insecurity. Individuals who have self-confidence usually also have a sense of "connectedness." On the other hand, if we're not sure that we like or accept ourselves, we will tend to expect others not to like or accept us either. This projection of our own negative feelings onto others around us can cause our prediction of being rejected to be fulfilled.

Brenda, a secretary in an office typing pool in a major northwestern city, had two close friends, Peggy and Lucille. Brenda suffered from severe PMS, which normally she was able to hide, but on one particularly bad day things just came apart for her at the office. She unloaded her irritability on both Peggy and Lucille by snapping at everything they said and complaining that she was doing more than her share of the work.

Peggy's sense of security and self-confidence, based on a strong sense of fellowship with Christ, enabled her to say, "Brenda's having a bad day today. I'll cut her some slack." Lucille, who was an intensely insecure and self-critical woman, personalized the attack, saying, "Now I know Brenda doesn't like me. Our friendship is over!"

Fellowship was easily restored between Peggy and Brenda, but Lucille's lack of confidence in herself made reconciliation a much more difficult matter. Since she also resented Peggy's defense of Brenda, a rift developed between Lucille and Peggy, too, causing feelings of loneliness.

Closely related to the loneliness linked to insecurity are dependency issues, which we will discuss in chapter 11 on "codependency." All too often a lonely individual waits for a special friend or perfect mate who will be his or her all-in-all. Such idealistic daydreaming surrenders control of one's moods and actions to someone else. Moreover, this kind of super-rescuer rarely exists outside of romance novels!

The Bitter Roots of Lonely Feelings

The fourth major cause of loneliness is bitterness, which usually includes a lack of forgiveness toward others. Nancy, for example, suffered severe emotional, physical, and sexual abuse by her father during her childhood. She has come to feel like "damaged merchandise" and is convinced that anyone who becomes aware of her past will automatically reject her. Nancy protects herself from the expected rejection by rebuffing any friendly overtures. She distrusts nearly everyone, yet feels intense loneliness. Rather than dealing with her own part in causing her lonely isolation, Nancy blames her father for *all* her problems and vows that she can never forgive him.

A harsh, bitter, unhappy individual, Nancy constantly rehearses in her mind—and verbally with the few people who can stand to be around her—just how terrible her life has been and what a monster her father is. Granted, from a human perspective, Nancy's father doesn't deserve her forgiveness. Yet the key point is that Nancy is punishing herself and blocking any healing by refusing to forgive. Her choice of bitterness rather than forgiveness (see Eph. 4:31–32) leaves Nancy an isolated and lonely person.

Inwardly Focused Anger

A fifth and often very subtle cause of loneliness involves feelings of false guilt and/or a lack of forgiveness toward self. Just as an individual may bear a sometimes unwarranted degree of anger toward others for their perceived wrongdoings, a lonely person may be carrying an exaggerated self-directed hostility for what is perceived as sins of his or her own. Even more tragically, the self-blame may be deeply hidden as well as unjustified (as in some cases of sexual abuse, where the victim finds imaginary reasons for partially blaming herself for the offenses perpetrated against her). Whatever the basis for the self-hatred—a general feeling of unworthiness or guilt over specific past sins—a vicious cycle of loneliness may become established.

As previously noted, guilt feelings for actual wrongdoing fractures fellowship with God and with others until the issue of the sin is resolved through confession and forgiveness. False guilt, however, is much more difficult to deal with. Counterfeit remorse involves feeling angry with yourself over perceived wrongs that have been labeled as such by personal, parental, ecclesiastical, or cultural injunctions rather than by Scripture.

Bruce Narramore and Bill Counts, authors of *Freedom from Guilt*, explain that "although the Bible discusses legal guilt and theological guilt, it never tells the Christian to feel psychological guilt." They further declare that, while the constructive sorrow of legal and theological guilt leads to repentance, psychological guilt leads to spiritual deadness and defeat.

Many Christians believe that due to their supposedly secure relationship with Christ, or their position in the church, they should never have psychological problems. Unlike counselor and church leader Les Carter (quoted earlier in this chapter), they never admit to feeling lonely, angry, or discouraged. This lack of transparency, which violates the instructions to confess our faults to one another for prayer (James 5:16) and to bear one another's burdens (Gal. 6:2), actually perpetuates any feelings of guilt, whether real or imaginary.

If we believers refuse to honestly share our burdens with others, we are burying our negative emotions and tend to give the false impression that we have no burdens. This may trigger feelings of false guilt in others, since they may then think, "I must be the only one who ever has problems with such-and-such. I must be worse than everyone else."

The Stress Factor of Holidays

How do the above-mentioned spiritual and psychological causes of loneliness relate to holiday depression? To the degree that holidays produce additional stress, they can exacerbate each of these elements. Holidays are times when we are usually extremely busy and thus may tend to ignore our relationship with God. Time pressures, financial concerns, travel, and temptations toward self-indulgence can cause our walk with the Lord to become a low-priority item. In similar fashion, though we are surrounded by people at holidays, both we and they are often so preoccupied that relationships and real communication needs may be ignored or neglected.

Partly because of often unrealistic ideas of how a holiday is *supposed* to be celebrated, failure to achieve that lofty standard, for whatever reason, may heighten any existing feelings of insecurity and underscore one's lack of self-confidence. Also, since holidays bring about renewed contact with family members and friends with whom we have had conflict in the past, feelings of bitterness and a lack of forgiveness toward those people may be brought to the surface. All these factors can contribute to our feelings of guilt and thus to the loneliness-related holiday depression we sometimes experience.

Resolving Holiday Loneliness

What can you do to overcome the lonely feelings that contribute to holiday depression?

1. *Make it a point not to let the holidays become an occasion for neglecting your relationship with the Lord.* Walking in obedience to God's Word, trusting him when you don't understand why certain things happen, meditating on Scripture, worshiping with God's people—*these* should be your top priorities at holiday times as well as at other points during the year. The presence of the fruit of the Spirit—love, joy, peace, longsuffering, gentleness, goodness, faith, meekness, and self-control (Gal. 5:22–23)—serves as a barometer for where you are in your walk with the Lord.

2. *Recognize who you are—a member of God's family.* Experience appropriate self-confidence based on your position in Christ and your abilities, not on how your performance is evaluated by others. If you are to love your neighbor as yourself, you must understand the proper significance of that self.

3. *Reach out lovingly to others.* Everyone needs people, especially at holidays. When Jesus referred to the Old Testament law to remind us to love our neighbors, he was talking about the kind of unconditional love that expressed itself in friendship and encouragement. The important question to ask is not, "Do I have good friends?" but "Am I being a good friend?" In *Worry-Free Living,* we describe five major characteristics of a good friendship: love, peace, open communication, mutual

improvement, and refreshment. As counselors, we frequently encourage people who complain about their loneliness to undertake the goal of building one or two close friendships and to do so by working on the art of listening, positively encouraging others, and developing a genuine interest in the lives of their friends.

4. *Remember that life here is simply a pilgrimage to be lived one day at a time.* There may be points at which you feel alone, perhaps due to circumstances you cannot overcome. Sally, for example, could not control the fact that shortly after she and her young husband had moved two thousand miles to the West Coast, he abandoned her to run away with another woman—an event that took place the week before Christmas. Left in a new city far from home, with little money, upcoming holiday bills, and a small child, Sally had to begin working immediately.

Sally *was* alone. But, because of her commitment to Christ, she decided to implement several steps to forestall and overcome loneliness. She became involved in a singles support group, sought counseling from our West Coast clinic, began attending a large church that had a special ministry to singles, and looked for opportunities to reach out to people. There were moments when Sally experienced intense holiday depression, but—as she told one of our counselors—"I know these feelings are only temporary, as long as I keep the Lord by my side."

The apostle Paul described life's afflictions as "light and momentary troubles" (2 Cor. 4:17), not to be compared with eternity in the presence of God and fellow believers, where loneliness will never be felt again. By adopting this long-term perspective, Sally was able to live one day at a time, even on the holidays that had brought her personal pain. Most importantly, she moved ahead with her life constructively, making scriptural choices to overcome her loneliness and heal her wounds. More than anything else, reaching out to other people helped whittle her burden of holiday depression down to a manageable size.

8

Seasonal Affective Disorder

Do you dread winter because you know you'll get depressed? Around October or November, do you begin feeling lethargic and craving carbohydrates? Then, as you gain weight and are less active, do you withdraw from people and stay indoors as much as possible? If you answered yes to these questions, read on. You may be experiencing seasonal affective disorder—SAD.

What Is SAD?

This group of symptoms differs from general depression in two important ways. First, as the name implies, SAD is directly related to the season of winter months. A person who feels fine throughout other seasons of the year will begin to feel down and depressed as winter approaches and the daylight hours shorten. Once the season changes into spring and days are longer once again, the feelings of depression begin to lift and may not return until the next winter.

Second, this period of seasonal depression must be recurrent to be correctly diagnosed as SAD. One case of "winter blahs" does not mean that seasonal affective disorder is the culprit. This depression, often severely debilitating, occurs every year within a roughly sixty-day period during mid-winter, then gradually clears up in one or two months as daylight periods get longer.

Before we label all depressive feelings during winter with the "seasonal affective disorder" tag, another possibility must be examined. Can these feelings of sadness and despair be related to a loss or other painful memory associated with the winter season? Consider Belinda, whose husband announced on Thanksgiving that he was homosexual and wanted a divorce. Belinda faced several difficult months of adjusting to the news. Even years later, Belinda could expect to feel depressed every winter. Such an emotionally devastating event is usually very difficult to deal with, even as time passes, and for Belinda every Thanksgiving would be a reminder of that tragedy. Since we all use some degree of denial to protect ourselves from emotional pain, denying the anniversary of a winter loss would not be unusual. However, if we wrongfully blame seasonal affective disorder for our depressive feelings, none of the suggestions offered later in this chapter will help. As already noted, sometimes emotional wounds must be opened up so that unresolved guilt, bitterness, and grudges can be drained off, forgiveness occur, and healing begin.

The third way in which SAD differs from general depression is related to light and darkness. Most people prefer sunny days over cloudy ones. Rarely do you hear someone say, "What a beautiful, sunny day; let's stay inside" or "Today is so cloudy and gray; let's go outside." Aside from learned likes and dislikes (we usually remember having more fun outdoors when the weather was bright and clear than when it was dismal), there is also a physiological reason for this preference.

The small pineal gland in the middle of the brain produces a hormone called *melatonin*. This is a very depressive secretion, and its production is regulated by the degree of natural light. The more darkness a person is exposed to, the more melatonin is produced, and the more depressed he or she will feel. Melatonin is a close cousin to the "feel good" hormone, *serotonin*, which serves as a neurotransmitter in the brain. Serotonin is also present in the pineal gland, but it can be converted to the depressive melatonin. (This conversion of serotonin to melatonin is not possible in other organs.)

David is an engineering consultant in his late forties. He accepted a job transfer from Florida to New York several years ago. Each winter since the move he has felt blue and listless. Because getting up each morning is a real effort, he is frequently late to work. Furthermore, when he is home he prefers to watch television or read rather than interact with family or friends. Does David have seasonal affective disorder? Probably yes.

According to Dr. Russell Reiter, a researcher and professor of anatomy at the University of Texas, San Antonio, SAD is an extreme case of what is commonly called cabin fever. This occurs when most of a person's time is spent sequestered from sunlight. The farther north (or south, in the southern hemisphere) one lives from the equator, the more common SAD is, because the hours of sunlight dramatically decrease in those regions. When David moved from Florida, whose warm, sunny weather invites outdoor winter activity, to New York, where hours of daylight are considerably less, and colder weather also encourages staying inside, his pineal gland worked overtime to produce the depressive hormone melatonin. Thus, David gradually felt more depressed as winter progressed.

Another aspect of the effect of light and darkness

on the pineal gland relates to reproductive physiology. Melatonin can be very sexually depressive, which explains why many outdoor animals can only reproduce at certain times of the year. The shortening winter days that increase production of melatonin lead to interference with female ovulation. When Lieutenant William Perry (later promoted to Admiral) returned from an expedition to the North Pole in 1907, he reported on the cessation of menstruation in Eskimo women during winter months, when limited light sources were available.

Light, specifically the color distribution of light, is the key to SAD. In reference to the pineal gland, fluorescent light is somewhat adequate, but natural sunlight is ideal. Special light kits are available that produce a wavelength distribution similar to sunlight. Although they are not as bright as the real thing, they are brighter and more effective than most artificial light.

Light therapy has been beneficial to some people with SAD. Dr. Normal Rosenthal of the National Institute of Mental Health in Bethesda, Maryland, has prescribed two hours of daily exposure to a bank of special lights that copy the wavelengths of visible and invisible sunlight. In his early research group, about two hundred adults with SAD were helped. Additional studies by other researchers have yielded similar encouraging results. However, these light kits are expensive and are not guaranteed to work for everyone. If such lights are flawed in design or used improperly, they can cause eye problems. Even worse, they can keep a person with a different type of depression or physiological disorder from getting proper treatment.

Such was the case with Bonnie, who felt anxious twenty-four hours a day and became very depressed in winter or on other days that were cloudy. Bonnie felt pressure against and within her body, experienced shortness of breath, and would cry easily. She hoped that light therapy would eliminate the depressive feelings of what a well-meaning friend had told her was probably SAD. Actually, since Bonnie suffered from the effects of a dysfunctional pineal gland, light therapy for her would be pointless. People who truly have seasonal affective disorder do not have problems with the pineal gland itself but with the ability to deal with insufficient light.

Who Is Susceptible to SAD?

What kind of person is likely to experience SAD? Adult women seem four times more likely than men to have this disorder. (Research is continuing into whether girls are more susceptible than boys.) When SAD does strike younger people, it seems to do so in the teen years.

Although living in areas where mid-winter days are very short could leave certain individuals more prone to SAD, other factors must also be considered. In Fairbanks, Alaska, for example, individuals have an average of only two or three hours of sunlight each winter day. They leave for work each morning in darkness and return home each evening the same way. In addition, the employment situation in parts of Alaska has been quite unstable. Other people, who work in jobs like construction or commercial fishing or on the oil pipelines, may be separated from their families for weeks on end. All these circumstances could provide additional causes for depression.

Boredom probably plays a role in seasonal affective disorder. Late winter is typically cold, gray, and bare—not a very exciting season compared to spring's greenery or autumn's abundance of color. Possibly the lack of stimulation during those months reminds us of other boring times in our lives and contributes to depression. That, plus the fact that bills from Christmas and IRS-related materials come rolling in about that time, may explain why February is the least favorite month of most Americans!

Dr. Meier has concluded from his counseling experience since living in the Dallas area that SAD is but one of several factors contributing to depression, accounting for perhaps as little as 20 percent of depressive feelings in this relatively southern area.

Dr. Verle Bell, psychiatrist with the Minirth-Meier Clinic in Chicago, practiced for years in Anchorage, Alaska. He agrees that SAD is typically a *contributor* to wintertime depression but suggests that rarely, if ever, is SAD the only cause for such depression. Dr. Bell has further observed that if a person *wants* to peg his depression on something physiological, he may say, "I have SAD." This may be the individual's way of denying that something more significant is going on psychologically. The reverse also holds true—if a person fears a medical reason for an ailment, he may resist seeing a doctor and claim the problem is purely psychological. We have observed that people tend to deceive themselves into believing the opposite of what is true, often to their own harm.

Self-Help for Seasonal Affective Disorder

If you believe you suffer from seasonal affective disorder, first check with a medical professional to rule out any organic causes for your depression. Is there a medical condition that could be a factor, such as anemia, thyroid dysfunction, or a side effect of medication? Once such possibilities have been eliminated, the best advice for people with SAD is to get as much natural sunlight as possible. Early morning hours are probably best. Avoid time in rooms with subdued lighting, which fails to adequately suppress production of melatonin. Break the cycle of withdrawal-depression-withdrawal by getting out, doing what you can, and maintaining active involvement with people. Certainly not all depressive symptoms are due exclusively to excess melatonin, but getting additional time in sunlight will not hurt a bit.

Be sure, also, to examine other emotional possibilities. Is winter the anniversary of a loss? Does it remind you of other boring or down times in your life? Does winter throw you into closer contact with someone toward whom you have unresolved negative feelings? After all, grudges are a known serotonin depleter. Are your financial concerns greater at this time?

Dr. Bell offers some final advice for people with SAD:

> Be aware of it. Stop using depression and fatigue as an excuse not to try. This is closely related to the issue of faith. We need to see ourselves as valuable persons who are granted, by God, to do certain things in life. Often he asks his servants to walk through those responsibilities even when depressed. Excusing yourself from those responsibilities and withdrawing will only make it worse. Instead, say, "Regardless of how I feel, as an act of reasonable sacrifice to my Lord, I will do what little I can." That will usually be enough to pull you through.

9

Holidays for Singles and Fragmented Families

Usually, when we think of holiday festivities, the people who come to mind are traditional family groups—Dad, Mom, two or three kids (and their pets), and perhaps a set or two of grandparents, with some aunts, uncles, and cousins mixed in for good measure.

Unlike the typical "Walton family" Christmas portrait, however, there are many individuals and groups who do not fit this mold. One national survey indicated that there are more than sixty-eight million single American adults. Many of these have never been married; others have been divorced or widowed. One of the largest subgroups in this category is the single parent. There are also the stepfamilies (or blended families), some of which are joined together in happy harmony, but others are racked by jealousy, conflict, and an ours-theirs mentality.

In our counseling experience we have discovered singles, single parents, and blended families to be uniquely at risk for holiday depression. In addition to the general issues that affect us all (such as those cited in previous chapters), these individuals face complexities of life that are particularly heightened and intensified at the holiday season.

Special People/Different Needs

Singles

The word *single* often carries a stereotyped image: a young adult, either never married or recently divorced, living a high-income yuppie lifestyle and enrolling in computer dating services! However, the singles group includes a wide range of people—from the never-married (of any age), to those divorced or widowed while still young, to more elderly widows, widowers, or divorced people.

For a large number of these individuals, Christmas is a time to be faced either alone or in the company of other singles and with minimal contact with a Norman Rockwell-type family. Although there may be a tree, tinsel, turkey, and trimmings, what is usually missing is the happy shouts of children, the gentle pleasure of seeing beloved family members, and the reminders they conjure of long-time traditions that warm the heart. Since holidays are, by cultural definition, joyous celebrations of happy togetherness, singles of all types are frequently set up for heightened emotions that are often sad or otherwise painful. Further complicating things for some singles may be relationships that are shallow rather than lasting and intimate. The single may be tempted to "put on a happy face" and pretend to be experiencing the joy of the occasion. Many times, though, such surface joy hides feelings of anguish over a recent divorce, business failure, or other kind of humiliation.

Coupled with the dilemma of not having "a significant other" is the fact that, because our society is so mobile, many singles live far away from family and long-term friends. Claudette, a magazine editor who had relocated to Los Angeles from the Midwest, talked about the problem of today's rootless society by saying, "Los Angeles isn't anything like my home town. It's taken me almost two years to begin to feel comfortable and blend in, but I have no really close friends. Furthermore, in Los Angeles almost everyone seems like a newcomer."

For many older singles, whether widowed or divorced, holiday travel to be with family is not possible because of health or financial limitations. Nettie, a widow of many years, lives in a northwestern city, hundreds of miles from her nearest relative. Many in her circle of friends spend holidays with their nearby families, leaving Nettie to spend the holidays alone most of the time. Limited income makes it even difficult for Nettie to phone faraway family members, who often are so caught up in their personal holiday activities that they neglect to phone her. The result is deep-seated loneliness, which (as we have seen) often leads to depression.

What would you imagine the homes of these two women to look like at Christmas? If you visited Claudette's apartment, you would find it decorated to the hilt with every Christmas trinket available, right down to the holly-print bathroom tissue. This could reveal a desperate attitude of "I'm going to have myself the merriest little Christmas ever, even if it kills my budget" (which the lavish parties she throws may well do).

On the other hand, Nettie's house shows no sign of the holiday, except a few greeting cards propped up on top of her television. Perhaps she feels that the sooner the holiday is over, the better. Nettie's successive years of lonely Christmases have taken away her desire to celebrate.

Those descriptions probably remind each of us of someone we know. Both scenarios illustrate the need for singles to keep a balanced perspective on the holidays. (There will be some suggestions toward that end later in this chapter.)

Single Parents

For single parents, holidays often heighten their sense of loss. Whether because of death or divorce, they are left attempting to be both father and mother to the kids. Jackie shares her frustration in this situation:

> I didn't ask to be a single parent. My ex-husband was abusive and an alcoholic. He left me, ran around for a while, and finally married another woman. Trying to raise three small children and have an outside job isn't easy most of the time, but it's particularly tough around Christmas and other holidays. Expenses are higher. The kids expect presents. Sometimes there's a sense of feeling I need to buy extra-nice presents to compete with their dad. He lavishes gifts on the kids around Christmas and new clothes around Easter to compensate for his delinquency in child-support payments throughout the rest of the year.
>
> It's also really tough for me to try to be both Dad and Mom to my son, Phillip—shooting baskets, repairing bicycles, and later trying to communicate with him about the facts of life.
>
> The kids go to their father's for Christmas, Easter, and other holiday visits—and things are always extra-traumatic when they return home. Discipline is out the window, expectations are running high, and I seem to be labeled the "bad parent."

Like Jackie, many single parents face ongoing difficulties, both practical and emotional, from the previous loss of a spouse. These complications heighten any residual sense of loss and may lead to bitterness, a key ingredient in holiday depression.

Maureen, a career single in her late thirties, had two small children. She had married her high-school sweetheart while very young. Following their marriage he had changed from an easygoing, compassionate companion to an irresponsible loafer who abandoned her and began living with someone else. Although Maureen sought to bring about reconciliation and pursued counseling, her husband filed for divorce and married the younger woman.

The local church in which Maureen had grown up placed a strong emphasis on Bible exposition and on "godly conduct," as defined quite narrowly. Sadly for Maureen, when she became "a divorced Christian," many of her former friends—and even some of her family who were active in the church—began shunning her. As she expressed it to her counselor, "It was as though I was the one at fault. I know every marital break-up has two sides, and I certainly wasn't perfect. But I needed their support, their help, and their love."

Unfortunately, some local churches, without regard for the tragic story behind many divorces, simply label even victimized now-single individuals as "unclean." The judgmental attitudes and resulting sense of isolation all too often can lead to despair. Similarly, singles who have never married are sometimes treated as though something is wrong with them because they have "failed to find a mate." This critical spirit may not be verbally expressed, but the underlying emotion can often be felt. Is it any wonder that singles, and especially single parents, tend to experience more holiday depression than average?

Blended Families/Second Marriages

When it comes to blended families, many people have the mistaken idea that—like in the old TV series "The Brady Bunch"—there are problems, but they can usually be solved rather quickly, with a little effort. While counseling parents of blended families we have observed that this is not the case. In fact, Dr. Paul Warren, head of our Child and Adolescent Division at the Minirth-Meier Clinic, points to the dynamics of the blended family as being a possible factor in a great deal of child and adolescent depression.

Frequently, when stepfamilies are formed, both spouses are still recovering from either the death of a mate or a divorce. They therefore often expect the other person to help compensate for past losses and "make things right." In addition, difficult adjustments and potential sources of conflict face every stepparent, including discipline issues, jealousy, and control of money. These and many other factors complicate the family dynamics. In some cases, both sets of children accuse the stepparent of favoring his or her biological children. Conversely, parents may seek to compensate for any partiality they may *feel* for their natural offspring by favoring their stepchildren, becoming very hard on their biological children in the process.

Even when there are no children involved, a previously widowed individual in a second marriage may set up unrealistic expectations in regards to the new spouse, based in part on an idealized memory of the deceased. Such unfair comparisons can be the source of conflict, especially around the holidays, when a sense of loss may reappear and memories of long-gone holidays may be rekindled.

Unresolved Grief. Another complicating factor that

can lead to holiday depression in blended families or second marriages in general is the failure of one or both parents (or a childless widow or widower) to work through the grief process over the previous marriage relationship. Whether it ended in death or divorce, a major life loss was sustained. Whenever such a loss occurs, we must work through the associated grief. The next chapter will deal extensively with working through such grief. Yet it should be recognized at this point that single parents and stepfamilies are particularly susceptible to its effects. Especially after a divorce, a great deal of guilt and even shame is associated with the past, as well as bitterness against all others who were involved.

Incomplete Bonding. Yet another factor heightening the potential for holiday depression in blended families is something we call incomplete bonding. A truly "blended" family will eventually bond to the point where possessions and relationships are not recognized as "theirs" or "ours." If this bonding has not completely occurred, conflict can increase around holidays and lead to deeper distress.

Bill and Betty had married in the summer, and everything seemed to start off just fine in their newly formed household. Betty had been divorced for three years. Bill's wife had died of cancer eighteen months before he married Betty. He had two teenage sons; she had two sons and a daughter. After moving into a large, old home with ample space for all, the family began work on relating to one another and developing a solid, unified core.

Things went rather well for a while, but around Thanksgiving the apparent family unity seemed to fall apart. Bickering and quarrels led to name-calling among the offspring. Both parents were accused of showing favoritism. As Christmas approached, what had previously been a happy household turned into a playing field for an outright family feud. Bill withdrew into his work. Betty became irritable and then severely depressed. The week before Christmas, her depression intensified until, by the time she came to see one of our counselors, Betty was almost dysfunctional.

The counselor wisely called a session for the entire family. At first, Bill refused to take time off from work, but finally a meeting was arranged with everyone—Mom, Dad, and the five youngsters. Accusations and counter-charges were hurled back and forth across the counseling room. Voices were raised in angry protest. Tears flowed. At one point Betty turned to the counselor and asked, "Do you see why I feel like giving up?"

Near the close of the session, Bill said, "I don't think we're getting anywhere. This is just making things worse."

The counselor replied, "I don't agree, Bill. I think what's happening is we're getting some of the family dynamics out in the open. Perhaps we can come up with a game plan to salvage this year's Christmas, and possibly create a foundation on which to build future holiday successes." Both Bill and Betty agreed to return the following week.

During the subsequent session the therapist zeroed in on a foundational issue that we have found to be crucial for blended families: the establishment of regular family conferences for open communication. The therapist encouraged Bill and Betty to read the book *Growing in Step* (Dan Houmes and Paul Meier [Grand Rapids: Baker, 1985]) and begin implementing the "Summit Meeting" plan explained therein. The therapist also described the benefits of family conferences. When held regularly, they can:

1. Provide family security
2. Stop hidden wedges from being driven between family members
3. Encourage the development of a healthy self-concept on the part of each family member
4. Furnish a forum for developing communication skills and learning problem-solving techniques
5. Create an atmosphere in which individual and family maturity could be developed

Incidentally, many families that have regular family conferences tend to neglect them around holidays because everyone is so busy. However, it is most important for the heavy holiday schedule not to preclude or hinder these meetings from taking place. Successful family conferences not only help blended families, but can be of tremendous use to any family group, especially in resolving the kinds of conflicts that may crop up at the holidays. These guidelines for "fighting fair" in a healthy Christian marriage can also help the entire family when worked through and applied.*

1. Sincerely commit your lives to Jesus Christ as Lord.
2. Consider the marriage a life-long commitment, just as Christ is eternally committed to his bride, the church.
3. Agree to always listen to each other's feelings, even if you disagree with the appropriateness of those feelings.
4. Commit yourselves to both honesty and acceptance.

*Most of these guidelines are based on "Successful Conflict Resolution in the Christian Life," unpublished counseling handout by Frank B. Wichern.

5. Determine to attempt to love each other *uncondi- tionally,* with each partner assuming 100 percent of the responsibility for resolving marital conflicts (the 50/50 concept seldom works).
6. Consider all the factors in a conflict before bringing it up with your mate.
7. Confess any personal sin in the conflict to Christ before confronting your mate.
8. Limit the conflict to the here and now—*never bring up past failures,* since all past failures should already have been forgiven.
9. Eliminate the following phrases from your vocabulary:
   a. "You never" or "You always"
   b. "I can't" (always substitute "I won't")
   c. "I'll try" (usually means "I'll make a half-hearted effort but won't quite succeed").
   d. "You should" or "You shouldn't" (these are parent-to-child statements)
10. Limit the discussion to the one issue that is the center of the conflict.
11. Focus on that issue rather than attacking each other.

Custody Considerations. A final factor that can contribute intensely to holiday depression for those in stepfamilies has to do with custody of the children involved. Few of the problems faced by blended families have as much potential to create emotional pain as shared custody or one-parent custody with visiting rights for the other parent. Sometimes divorced parents wind up alternating holidays with their children, thus missing certain special occasions. The emotional ups and downs caused by having the children present for one holiday and then absent for another adds both sadness and stress. Further complicating the picture can be jealousy and/or the influence exercised by the other parent, particularly if the two parents' values differ.

Bill and Betty found their lives impacted at holidays by this factor because Betty's children were required to spend some holidays with her ex-husband. The book *Growing in Step* contains important guidelines for dealing with these issues, yet counseling is often necessary to help bring about resolution of the emotions associated with custody and visitation rights.

Holiday Helps for "Special People"

One important principle for resolving holiday depression focuses on plans in which an individual or an entire family becomes involved in reaching out to help someone less fortunate. *Any* family (or group of single friends) can undertake projects in which goods are collected to give to people in need or whose aim is to share in other appropriate ways with shut-ins and the lonely elderly, for example. For the last fifteen years, the family of one of the authors has put together baskets of presents to be left on Christmas Eve at a holiday mission for delivery to selected families or individuals. Sharing in projects that intrinsically reflect a spirit of love and giving helps cut down on some of the jealousy and bitterness that surfaces around the holidays in too many self-centered souls!

Families, blended or otherwise, can reach out to singles and single-parent families by incorporating them into holiday activities. A shared Easter Sunday dinner, followed by a drive in the country to observe the arrival of spring blossoms—or a Labor Day cookout with home-made ice cream, horseshoes, and volleyball—can help these individuals nip holiday despair in the bud by showing them that someone cared enough to include them.

For the single parent, recognizing and accepting the limitations relative to the holidays is of great importance. One person cannot possibly be the perfect Mom *and* Dad. Even though there is a natural tendency to attempt this, the single parent needs to deal honestly with the limitations in his or her situation. Often counseling can help, and support groups for single parents provide encouragement and friendship that can be quite constructive. (Most successful single parents also know that enlisting the aid of a relative or other trusted friend of the opposite sex can enrich their children's lives by taking on some of the "recreational" responsibilities of the missing parent, both at holidays and throughout the year.)

The single parent must also recognize that seldom, if ever, will a "Prince [or Princess] Charming" appear to establish another lasting relationship. To think that remarriage will bring about the resolution of all the complications and difficulties faced by the single parent is to swallow a fairy tale. For single parents, holiday depression can be resolved in the same way difficulties at other times of the year are—by learning to live one day at a time with the peace, joy, and grace that only God can give.

The words of Jesus given thousands of years ago as part of the Sermon on the Mount carry tremendous practical implications for the single parent today in terms of the material, emotional, and spiritual needs of life. Single parents can easily become too focused on providing the necessities of life, especially at the holiday season. Furthermore, worry over the future can become an emotionally crippling factor. Memorizing, meditating on, and applying selected verses from Matthew 5–7 (especially Matt. 6:25–34) can offer significant help.

For the single individual, taking the initiative by

reaching out and planning to spend the holiday with friends or other family members can help keep such occasions from being emotionally devastating. Claudette, the magazine editor (after realizing that overspending was not the answer), put together a simple Christmas buffet for several friends, and later went for a drive to look at holiday decorations with them. Eric, another single, has become involved in feeding the homeless at a rescue mission over the Christmas holiday. He also plans to phone two or three friends and relatives from whom he is separated on the holidays.

These and other singles agree that a number-one antidote for holiday loneliness and depression is to reach out in helping others. As Terry, a musically gifted single, put it, "There are all kinds of people who like the music of Christmas and Easter. Our choir group always enjoys going to nursing homes, hospitals, and retirement centers to cheer people up—and we are really the ones who are cheered up the most!"

What Terry expressed is consistent with the words of Jesus: "Give, and it will be given to you. A good measure, pressed down, shaken together and running over, will be put into your lap. For with the measure you use, it will be measured to you" (Luke 6:38).

All of us—whether singles, single parents, stepparents, or part of a traditional family—can look for ways to *give* emotionally. With Christ's help, we can reach out to others and be willing to give as well as receive love and encouragement (1 Thess. 5:11; Heb. 3:13). In doing so, we are often able to blunt the sharp edge of holiday loneliness and depression for others—and for ourselves.

10

Loss, Grief,
and the Holiday Effect

To most people who knew them, Peter and Phyllis were the epitome of a devout and well-adjusted couple. They had happy children and a comfortable home in the suburbs. Busy though they were in professional and family-oriented matters, they stayed active in both the community and a local evangelical church. Not only did Peter and Phyllis have few material concerns, they seemed to have it all together. However, two years ago, right before the Christmas holidays, one of their three children died in a traffic accident. Naturally, this event shook the family profoundly, but they apparently worked through their grief and began to heal. By the next fall, things seemed to be back on an even keel.

But the remaining son continued to grieve over his brother's death. Some of the grief was caused by guilt (the survivor was driving the car) and anger (because he missed his brother). So on Christmas morning of that year, he took a gun from his father's collection, left a suicide note, and ended his life.

The family was terribly shaken by this second loss, and Phyllis became so depressed that her brain chemistry was altered to the extent that she lost touch with reality. When she came to the Minirth-Meier hospital unit, she was greatly at risk for suicide herself. Ultimately, through intensive individual therapy for Phyllis, group counseling for the rest of the family, and the support and fellowship of the church family and other loving friends, Phyllis, Peter, and their remaining child recovered. But even so, Christmas celebrations for this family will always be tinged with sadness.

The experience of Phyllis and Peter reminds us of an important observation about depression: during holidays or other times, depression is often a direct result of unresolved grief. As Dr. Archibald Hart asserts in his book *Coping with Depression in the Ministry and Other Helping Professions*, "All reactive depression can be understood as a response to some kind of loss."

Types of Loss

The term *loss* has many connotations. It can refer to a bereavement or negative change in circumstances, a perception that one's situation has changed for the worse (though that may not actually be the case), or an anticipatory mind-set that a loss will occur in the foreseeable future.

Real Loss

Whether we lose a loved one to cancer, or a job as a result of a hostile corporate takeover, or a large sum of money due to a bank or business failure, or a spouse because of divorce or an extramarital affair, or a child as a runaway, or our self-esteem because someone's malicious gossip has destroyed our reputation, we experience grief over whoever or whatever is now missing in our lives.

Some losses—like the loss Peter and Phyllis experienced when two children died over a relatively short period—are real, tangible, and concrete. Though we may realistically accept the inevitability of death, we grieve nonetheless. When someone we know dies, we lose contact and fellowship with that person.

On a less dramatic scale, when geography limits our contact with a loved one or when a marital connection is severed, there is a changed quality of life that can likewise produce a sense of grief. And downward trends in financial status often call up a feeling of what is now missing in terms of our ability to spend on personal needs and wants. All "losses," to one degree or another, can be expected to produce grieving reactions. How we handle them will determine our mental state and lifestyle in general.

Perceived Loss

However, other feelings of loss are more subtle. Perhaps an adult child has gone through a traumatic divorce and we share in the child's loss vicariously. For example, Susan's daughter, who had been married three years and had two small children, had married a man who came from a dysfunctional background and was also an alcoholic. Because of his persistent abuse, Susan's daughter found it necessary to separate and eventually obtain a divorce. Not only did Susan feel extremely responsible for not properly teaching her daughter to make a wiser choice in a husband, she also believed that a marital failure made her daughter less than a conscientious Christian. From that reasoning, Susan came to the conclusion that she had lost status as a "conscientious" parent. (The daughter had also become somewhat embittered toward God during the process of the abuse she suffered and the breakup of her marriage.) Susan, perceiving that she had somehow failed to do a worthwhile job as a mother in the eyes of God and others, began to grieve unduly over her own shortcomings and loss of prestige and soon became depressed.

Potential Loss

Sometimes the "loss" we experience may not fit either of these categories because it involves what we *expect* to occur. When Robert was told that his father had developed terminal cancer of the prostate, he began to have difficulty functioning at work. He withdrew into himself and became cynical at home. Although he would not admit it, he was severely depressed. While his father was still undergoing treatment for cancer and actually had the possibility of recovery, Robert was already feeling the potential loss of his dad and became involved in a grief syndrome. An anticipated loss, which may never actually happen, can be just as debilitating as a real or perceived loss. Exaggerated worries over possible negative events in the future can also cause depressive reactions.

Grief and Holiday Depression

Perhaps at this point you are asking, "What is the relationship between grief and holiday depression?" After all, not everyone suffers grief at the holidays as Peter and Phyllis did. The answer can be seen in the fact that depression, or feelings of grief, frequently runs in cycles, or a series of stages. Since holidays are commemorative occasions, they often recall to mind past events, even if they are not specifically associated with that particular season. Especially where the loss of a family member is recalled, the stages of grief connected with that situation may be re-experienced, often with depressive effects. These stages, briefly described in chapter 3, have been carefully documented in the book *Happiness Is a Choice.* They are as follows:

Stage 1: Denial. When a loss occurs, our first and most normal reaction is usually a statement of disbelief. We may say, "I don't believe it," or "Surely you must be wrong!" In psychiatric and pastoral practice, we have often had the responsibility of telling individuals about the death of a loved one or about some other loss. Almost invariably the response is "Are you sure? I can't believe it. I never thought it would come to this. Can't something be done?" Frequently, those who are in this state of shock or denial experience a feeling of numbness or unreality. This initial stage of grief may last for hours. In other cases it may last for days or for much longer periods.

People in the denial stage of grief may react in totally different ways. For example, Gene, who was in his sixties, was laid off from his factory job as shift supervisor less than a year before he was to have retired with full benefits. Although he refused to talk to anyone about how he felt, he acted as if he believed he would be reinstated momentarily. Doris, on the other hand, who lost her home and one of her children in a tornado, immediately began talking incessantly about a wide variety of mostly unrelated subjects. Both Gene and Doris were denying their losses.

We have seen individuals in the denial stage who seemed totally drained of energy, virtually catatonic and unable to move. Others have thrown themselves into a whirlwind of domestic or other tasks, exhibiting intensive energy. Some have talked pleasantly and dreamily of heaven when a loved one died. Others have said, "It's not possible that God would take him away from me." All of these patterns are ways we manifest the denial stage of grief.

In a classic biblical account of loss suffered from death, Jesus' raising of Lazarus, we find a number of the stages of grief illustrated, including denial. When Jesus told his disciples in figurative terms, "Our friend Lazarus has fallen asleep; but I am going there to wake him up" (John 11:11), the response of the disciples was, "Lord, if he sleeps, he will get better" (v. 12). John explains that Jesus spoke of Lazarus's death, yet the others continued to think he had spoken of taking rest in sleep (v. 13). What we have in these verses appears to be misperception on the part of the disciples, perhaps coupled with denial. Jesus finally breaks through the denial by stating plainly, "Lazarus is dead" (v. 14).

Stage 2: Anger Turned Outward. As the reality of the experienced loss begins to penetrate, the emotions within the individual begin to surface. The most common emotional side effect of grief is anger. This is appropriate, since anger, by definition, is a hostile response to a real or perceived threat or loss.

Sometimes the anger is directed toward the person who brought the news of the loss. Duane, for example, lashed out at the policeman who told him his brother had been killed in a traffic accident by saying, "How dare you tell me this! What kind of uncaring person are you to be so calm?" On other occasions, the anger is focused on the medical profession, such as the doctors and nurses who cared for the individual who died. The grieving person may declare, "If the doctors had really been on top of her case, they would have found the cancer before it spread and she wouldn't have died."

The mourner may even express anger toward the person who died. This cannot always be understood or verbalized, but the feeling is, "You died and went off and left me here." One young widow who was left with three small children said to her pastor at the funeral home, "I know I shouldn't, but I just feel angry at him because he's in heaven and I have to take care of these kids, pay the bills, and somehow try to cope with life."

This stage of grief also almost always involves some anger toward God for allowing the loss to occur. In a sense, this is the kind of feeling Martha was sharing with Jesus when she said, "Lord, if you had been here, my brother would not have died" (John 11:21). Her sister, Mary, later expressed the same kind of feeling (v. 32).

Apologist C. S. Lewis was a bachelor for many years. He married later in life but soon after lost his wife to cancer. Writing under a pseudonym, Lewis, though strong in faith, expressed, "Oh God, God, why did you take such trouble to force this creature out of its shell if it is now doomed to crawl back—to be sucked back—into it?" Anger toward God has been felt even by such godly persons as Job or contemporary Christians like Lewis.

Stage 3: Anger Turned Inward (Guilt). In the process of grieving, the person who suffered the loss will usually move next into the state of feeling personally responsible for that loss. This is partly because guilt quite naturally follows anger. It represents the emotion of anger pushed inward upon ourselves because of actual or perceived wrongdoing. In the case of actual wrongdoing, we call it *true guilt;* in the case of perceived wrongdoing, we call it *false (or unjustified) guilt.* The guilt phase of grief may be a combination of both types, but it is typically false or exaggerated.

This stage ("anger turned inward") usually follows the second stage ("anger turned outward"), because having or expressing anger toward others or God often leaves us feeling guilty. This kind of guilt may be expressed in such statements as, "I didn't spend enough time with him. If only I had told him I loved him one more time."

Millie's husband, Tim, had been a successful business-man for many years. After suffering a number of reverses in the stock market and in real estate, he suf-fered a heart attack and died within a matter of weeks. As she mourned his death, Millie became stuck in the guilt phase of grief, feeling acutely responsible as she wondered over and over what she could have done to keep Tim from making those bad financial decisions. For example, Millie repeatedly told herself, "If he hadn't had to support me, he wouldn't have gotten in that financial shape. I probably cost him his life."

Usually the "anger turned inward" phase will involve some true guilt, since no relationship is perfect. Often there will be unresolved issues from the past, some of them relatively small, others quite significant. In cases like this, the person experiencing true guilt should acknowledge what he has done wrong, perhaps to a pas-tor, counselor, or friend. This is important and is pre-cisely what James calls for when he says, "Therefore confess your sins to each other and pray for each other so that you may be healed" (James 5:16).

On the other hand, much of what an individual feels at this time can be accurately termed false guilt. This involves holding unreasonable grudges against ourselves over things for which we are actually not responsible. False guilt can best be resolved by restructuring our thinking to avoid overpersonalizing or exaggerating the role we played in the events that preceded or indirectly led to the loss.

This particular stage of grief, although not specifically described in the account of Lazarus's death and resur-rection, is alluded to in Martha's statement: "But I know that even now God will give you whatever you ask"

(John 11:22). Without reading into Martha's mind what we are not told, the possibility exists that she felt, "If I had only prayed more." In our ministries we have heard many people make statements similar to Martha's words, which mask guilt feelings of "I didn't pray enough. Therefore, my loved one died."

Sometimes individuals will become stuck between Stages 2 and 3, alternating between periods of outwardly directed anger and inwardly projected grief. This is also the point at which many people will move into a "bargaining stage," saying, "God; if only you will _____, then I will _____."

Stage 4: Genuine Grief. Properly understanding and dealing with the aforementioned preliminary stages of grief can move a person toward the all-important fourth stage: genuine grief, meaning "pure" grief relatively uncomplicated by the other emotions. It is at this point that the grieved individual, whether reacting to death or to some other severe loss, begins to experience emotional catharsis, principally through the release of tears. From years of experience in psychiatric and pastoral practice, the authors strongly believe that anyone who suffers a significant loss should have a good cry. Sometimes a number of sessions with tears may be necessary to fully express the pain.

Unfortunately, our society has long proclaimed, "Big boys don't cry—and maybe big girls shouldn't either." Too often, through a well-meaning but misguided interpretation of verses like 1 Thessalonians 4:13, people are told to resist the impulse to cry openly. One young wife, in the midst of grief over the loss of a close family member, was told by her husband, "If you're going to cry, do it alone because I don't want to hear it." This husband, denying his own grief, later verbally lashed out with, "Stop crying, or I'll give you something to cry about."

Although such barbed comments are painful to those who wish to express their grief by appropriate crying, even more difficult to deal with are the assertions that it is unbiblical to cry. Some Christians mistakenly believe that the apostle Paul said Christians should not sorrow over "those who fall asleep [die]" (1 Thess. 4:13). Such a perspective is inaccurate. What Paul was actually saying here is: "We do not grieve *in the same way* as those who have no hope." He does not say, "We do not grieve." Paul was drawing a contrast between the despairing, irreversible grief of those who do not have the hope of eternal life available through faith in Christ and the painful yet short-term grief of those who, though saddened by loss, can nonetheless look ahead to the joyful prospect of being reunited with loved ones in the presence of the Lord.

When asked to memorize a Bible verse as children in Sunday school, many of us might have selected John 11:35 because of its brevity alone. This verse, however, carries a profound message concerning grief resolution: it affirms the validity of genuine sorrow and gives us permission to grieve: "Jesus wept."

Two short, simple words—yet words fraught with meaning. In the context, Martha seems to have had difficulty with tears. She can talk. She can question. She expresses her faith. She can encourage Mary to visit the Master (John 11:28), yet she apparently cannot cry. Mary, on the other hand, wept (v. 31), and so did those who followed her to the tomb where Jesus was waiting (v. 33). Feeling the human pain of losing his friend Lazarus and empathizing with the intense emotions that both sisters must have felt (although at this point only Mary was capable of expressing them through tears), *Jesus himself wept.* Even though he was the Son of God—omnipotent and thus *able* to raise Lazarus from the dead; omniscient and therefore *knowing* what he was about to do—Jesus wept.

May we never be guilty of discouraging weeping on the part of someone who has suffered a loss, particularly a death. Rather, may we give the bereaved permission to shed those healing tears of grief. Weeping, particularly to express grief in the face of death, is not only appropriate but necessary. Joe Bayly, who experienced the death of three sons, wrote the following in *The View from a Hearse* (Elgin, Ill.: David C. Cook, 1969, p. 15):

> We cannot beautify death. We may live with it and accept it, but we cannot change its foul nature. The apostle Paul spoke of death as an enemy, the last enemy to be destroyed. Death is the enemy of God, of man made in God's image. . . . Death wounds us, but wounds are meant to heal and, given time, they will.

Stage 5: Resolution. When a person has been able to work through grief and break through depression by getting in touch with feelings of anger both outward and inward and finally experiencing the emotional release of a "good cry," grief usually reaches its resolution. Here, healing can occur over time. Although a lingering sense of loss may remain, any self-destructive emotions can be understood and handled constructively. Life can proceed, though differently than before. Sometimes this happens quickly. Often it takes more time. Just when this stage is reached is affected by many factors, including one's personality, cognitive perception of the loss, self-concept, and the support received from friends.

Cycles of Grief Reactions

In terms of holiday depression, an important point to remember is that grief tends to run in cycles. Few depressive sorrowings follow the strict pattern set forth in the previously described stages. The process of grief resolution will often be marked by setbacks or by movement back and forth between a variety of stages. Two particular events tend to cause either repetition or stalling at one of the different stages of grief. These are the anniversary of the loss and certain holidays.

For example, the first Christmas following the death of a loved one is especially difficult for the spouse and other family members. Often the individual who died has been idealized, as have past events involving that person. Awareness of the empty place at the table, the absence of certain presents under the Christmas tree, and other missing ingredients tends to heighten the sense of loss related to the holidays.

Ruby and Sam had been married for twenty-two years when Sam developed unexplained pain during the Christmas season. He postponed going to the doctor until several weeks after the holidays. When he finally went, the diagnosis was cancer. Sam lived until summer. Ruby and the children seemed to bear up well immediately following his death and were handling the adjustment bravely until several weeks before Christmas. At that point, one of the children began acting out his pain by running with a fast teenage crowd, shoplifting, getting into fights, and using alcohol and drugs. Another child became highly anxious and agitated and was unable to sleep at night. Ruby began to experience exhaustion and intense feelings of depression. Even though this family's loss had not occurred precisely at Christmas, these individuals were experiencing grief-related holiday depression.

Herman and Sandra had a rather stormy decade of marriage. Their two young children watched as the marriage completely deteriorated over the period between

Thanksgiving and Christmas one year. The week before Christmas, Sandra stormed out of the house, saying, "I've had it. This marriage is over." Taking the children with her, she went "home to Mother." Within a few months the marriage had ended in an acrimonious divorce. For years thereafter, the immediate and extended family experienced holiday depression around Christmas.

Keith and Loretta finally fulfilled a lifelong dream of buying a house in the country. They painstakingly restored and decorated the place until it matched their shared mental picture of a perfect country home. A year later, they returned from an Easter weekend visit with relatives to find their home burned to the ground. From that point on, Easter became tainted by memories of the loss they had experienced.

Even if the major loss did not occur precisely on a holiday, remembering and re-experiencing the feelings of grief and loss from that time is all too common. This is particularly true with the holiday closest to the loss or immediately following it. As the examples cited in this chapter show, life's tragedies can strike at any time, and holidays are not exempt from their cruel blows.

Failure to grieve or work through these losses will often lead to depressive thoughts permeating one's consciousness: "Well, this is the holiday I lost my child." "Christmas will always be remembered as the season of our divorce." "Easter is the time when our house burned down, and we lost all those treasures we had collected." "This is the first holiday I haven't been with my children or grandchildren." "I'm spending Christmas alone this year instead of with my former mate."

When our focus at holiday times is on loss, it indicates that we have not yet worked through the entire grief process. Holiday depression is usually the result.

Whether we face and verbalize our feelings, seek counsel, receive encouragement from close friends, or educate ourselves with books and workshops on the subject, fully working through the grief associated with loss is vitally important. Doing so helps insulate us from bouts of grief-related holiday depression and keeps us moving ahead all through the year.

11

Codependency and Multigenerational Factors

Hiram and Mabel were their names. Virtually everyone who knew Hiram recognized that he was an alcoholic. Hiram had no particular drink of choice, but he usually came home every day with a "buzz." Holidays were particularly marked by the chaos that usually accompanies heavy drinking.

Most people considered Mabel a saint. Her pastor once said, "I seldom see anyone bear up under so much adversity, yet work as hard for Christ as Mabel does." Somehow she shepherded her three children through their father's drinking disasters, holiday turmoil, and other family upsets. Mabel had learned this coping strategy well, because both of her parents were alcoholics.

The three children, Bud, Becky, and Brian, somehow made it through school and seemed to overcome the traumas of a difficult family life. Bud, in fact, finished college (dean's list, graduation with honors, numerous extracurricular activities) and began preparing for the ministry. Brian, the youngest, seemed to do okay, too.

He was involved in drama in high school and was so clever with jokes and puns that some people considered him to have the makings of a professional comedian. Becky, on the other hand, ran with a fast crowd in school, became pregnant (the baby was put up for adoption), and finally left home to live with a boy her parents called "a worthless nobody."

From the outside, not everyone recognized the problems of this family. Many people knew that Mabel and the kids had been faithful in church for years and figured that her husband just didn't have time for church. After all, shift work at the local factory made regular church attendance difficult for a lot of men in the community. Others, who knew them better, were aware of Hiram's drinking problem and how Mabel and the kids tried to hold things together.

However, when the couple came to see a family counselor at the Minirth-Meier Clinic about some of the problems associated with Becky's self-destructive behavior, the therapist uncovered a web of problems extending throughout the family and stretching back into past generations. You see, the members of this family were "codependent." They were victims of Hiram's alcoholism, yet in subtle ways had contributed to his addiction.

What Is Codependency?

Codependency is a term used to describe the attitude and actions of the spouse (and other family members) in relation to a nonfunctioning member of the family unit, most often an alcoholic. For example, an alcoholic becomes the center of focus as the other family members learn to deny, cover up, and suppress their feelings about the problem. Everything a codependent feels is related to the activities and approval of the significant other. These are some of the "rules" a codependent person may follow:

1. It's not okay to talk about problems.
2. Feelings should not be expressed openly.
3. I must be strong, right, perfect.
4. I must not ever think of my own interests.
5. It's not okay to play or have fun.
6. I must not rock the boat.

A codependent person or an approval addict cannot personally turn on the inner light of feeling good about himself unless he has another do it for him. He can endorse himself only when someone he respects approves him first. He actually gives another person the power to control his feelings. An individual has a dependency disease or addiction when his dependency on others is on a "need" level. Sometimes the dependency is on another's dependency. In other words, "I need to be needed."

Since alcohol abuse is one of the major problems among adult males in America today, the attention of the counseling community has been focused on the concept of codependency. According to Dr. Timmon Cermak, president of the National Association for Children of Alcoholics, the concept first received attention as an outgrowth of the founding of AA and Al-Anon.

In the book *Love Is a Choice*, Dr. Robert Hemfelt describes the concept of codependency in terms of a four-layer cake. As we examine the cake from above, the top or most apparent layer involves the specific symptoms of the maladjustment, which may take the form of drug and/or alcohol abuse, workaholism, rage-aholism, obsessive-compulsive disorders, or sexual fixations such as an exaggerated attraction to pornography.

The second layer is composed of the associated faulty relationships. A young tree struck by lightning may survive the initial injury, but its branches grow twisted and skewed. So may familial and other significant relationships involving a dysfunctional individual become distorted.

The third layer involves a codependent's emotional pain, produced by some form of abuse. The abuse may have been obvious, as blatant as frequent beatings, incest, or sexual molestation. Or it could have been more subtle, such as parental abandonment due to divorce or neglect because of their workaholism. In any case, emotional pain is present in the life of a codependent because of some kind of past or present abuse in the family of origin.

Beneath this third component lies the core layer—basic love hunger. Each human being was born with the capacity to love and be loved. Dr. Hemfelt pictures this love hunger with a love tank. Every newborn has been issued a love tank, a reservoir waiting to be filled and thus able to release its supply to others. Normally, mothers and fathers are the first people to begin filling their child's love tank. As the child grows and develops, others may contribute in varying degrees. The major force behind the process is God, the ultimate source of love—" . . . love comes from God. . . . We love because he first loved us" (1 John 4:7, 19).

However, when the family in which a child originates is marked by volatile or unstable relationships, compulsive behavior or addictions, there is an improper balance between dependence and independence. Since both parents frequently have depleted love tanks themselves, they are unable to fill the child's reservoir. Furthermore, as the child grows older, the love-starved parents may attempt to refill their own empty tanks from the child's meager supply.

In such a situation, accurately described by some as "emotional incest," the behavior and attitude on the part of parents can leave lasting emotional scars (layer 3), distort future relationships (layer 2), and leave symptoms of devastation, such as workaholism and other addictions (layer 1), in the lives of those so abused. Individuals who grow up in homes where one or both parents were chemically addicted may vehemently assert, "I'll never let it happen to me." Yet these assertions are often belied by a strong tendency to do that very thing in an attempt to ease the long-term emotional pain.

Holiday Depression, Layer by Layer

How does codependency relate to holiday depression? Going back to the picture of the four-layer cake, we discover that holiday depression can be triggered at each of the four levels.

At the top level, symptoms of *any* kind of addiction can intensify during holidays, whether it be loneliness, burnout, unfulfilled expectations, idealized memories, or the like. Hiram didn't consider himself to be an alcoholic because three beers a day was his *usual* quota. But at holidays Hiram felt free to "tie one on" with his buddies. After all, he rationalized, a three- or four-day weekend gave him the chance to unwind that he "deserved." His family was left with the consequences, which ranged from (merely) his absence from holiday togetherness to stumbling bouts of unjustifiable rage when he returned.

In similar fashion, the characterization of Ebenezer Scrooge in Charles Dickens's *A Christmas Carol* shows how holidays can intensify the work addiction in the life of a workaholic. Symptoms that might be tolerable most of the time can become hopelessly intensified around holidays and lead to depression.

At the second level, relationships already distorted by the web of codependency become strained even further during holiday seasons. We have already documented the role that flawed relationships play in holiday depression. When codependency is present, that relationship factor is increased exponentially.

As for the third level, it should be noted that holidays are periods when abuse (which may be present but somewhat restrained at other times) can flare up and create a major problem. Albert was "a very nice guy" with an explosive temper and could easily be characterized as a rage-aholic. Most of the time Albert was able to keep his intense feelings of anger under control. Holidays, when Albert was home and around the family for longer periods of time, triggered explosions of seemingly mindless rage. Already pressured by seasonal downturns in his landscaping business, Albert's tolerance level was breached by what he considered the shortcomings of his family in meeting the exaggerated standards he had set for them. During his angry episodes, Albert beat his wife, threatened his children, broke furniture and dishes, and occasionally punched holes in drywall. Needless to say, this pattern triggered severe holiday depression for his wife and avoidance behavior on the part of his children.

At the fourth level, that core of love hunger in each of us is something that we tend to ignore, at least consciously, most of the time. But holidays, especially the more sentimental ones like Christmas, Mother's Day, or Father's Day, are times when the emotional hunger pangs of unmet love-needs can feel as painful as the physical hunger of a person who is twenty-four hours into a three-day fast.

The Dynamics of Codependency

The relationship between certain key characteristics of codependency and holiday depression can often be understood as a dysfunctional pattern of living for all those concerned. Though the person or family may appear strong, or at least stable, to others, they may be experiencing confusion and intense dependency as well as a sense of being trapped in a no-win situation. Family weaknesses are not to be made known to others. The impulse is to "stick together and keep up appearances." This takes a great deal of emotional energy, especially at otherwise tense holiday periods. As we have seen, energy depletion is one factor in holiday depression.

Codependency implies a lack of balance between interdependence with (and responsibility for) others and accountability for one's own actions—a balance clearly described in Galatians 6:1–6. In verse 2, Christians are exhorted to help carry one another's burdens or overload. We are not to be isolated from others who have needs, because Christ has mandated that we care genuinely for others. Paul hastens to add the counterbalance with a term that indicates the kind of personal backpack carried by a hiker or soldier: "For each one should carry his own load" (v. 5).

When codependency is present, boundary distortions occur. Someone (usually the spouse of the person with the addiction or other dysfunction) takes on the role of "rescuer" or enabler, futilely attempting to resolve the family's problems through sheer personal effort. Even children can fall into the twisted game of trying to "make up for Daddy's sickness" or "cure Mama's sadness." When coupled with the other pressures brought on by holidays, such well-meaning compensatory efforts can increase the sense of frustration and thus the likelihood for holiday depression to occur.

A major factor in depression, holiday or otherwise, is low self-esteem. Especially in codependent families, self-esteem of a family member is often principally derived through his or her ability to solicit the approval of one or more of the others (conditional love). This can lead to an attempt to fill a stereotyped family role.

The family "hero" may set out to prove that "Although Dad is a loser, I can overcome this rotten situation and win Mom's approval at the same time." The family "villain" establishes his place in the family hierarchy by creating his own self-fulfilling prophecy of failure: "What's the use? My mom's done some terrible things. I'm her son, so I must be pretty terrible, too." The family "clown" gains acceptance (and copes) by providing humor as an outlet for the emotional pain present. Finally, there is the "lost child" who simply doesn't seem to count. He or she is physically there but appears to "get lost in the cracks." This child is rarely a problem—just not much of anything—and usually feels like a nobody.

Family role playing in an attempt to bolster one's self-image is often intensified around the holidays. The "hero" must be *super*-human; the "villain" does worse things than usual to attract attention; the "clown" goes to greater lengths to entertain everyone gathered for holiday celebrations. The "lost child" redoubles his or her efforts not to "make trouble for anyone" and becomes even less noticed. Since none of these codependent roles are ever played perfectly, the actors experience a sense of failure, which equates with "loss." The result can be depression.

Since depression often results when powerful emotions are turned inward, family members who seek to adhere rigidly to these kinds of rules are setting themselves up (and each other) for great unhappiness, holiday and otherwise. Take, for example, rule five, "It's not okay to play or have fun." As noted in chapter 2, God's original "purpose" in permitting holidays was to provide occasions for joyful celebration. Obviously, if a problem-plagued family operates by the unwritten but rigidly enforced rule that *all* fun or play is taboo, conflict is instituted, leading to even more unhappiness at holiday times.

Is There a Cure?

Codependency is not easily overcome. Since there are so many factors interacting in most codependent relationships, there is no "six-step, quick-cure" counseling approach that guarantees a solution. Codependency is a web of bondage from which, as Jesus pointed out, only the truth liberates (John 8:32). Those involved in codependent families must first break through their denial and other defense mechanisms and identify both the extent of the problem and the actual cost in terms of emotional pain. Therapeutic knives must slice through all four layers in order to (1) deal directly with the negative symptoms/addictions; (2) restructure distorted relationships; (3) recognize the pain caused by previous abuse; and (4) ultimately find through God and significant others the missing love upon which self-esteem is formulated.

The key spiritual approach to overcoming the problems associated with codependency is to provide insight into the tangled web of false assumptions and faulty relationships that underlie the phenomenon. Especially strategic is communicating the important balance between bearing our personal burdens (responsibility) and the assistance we are to provide in bearing the burdens of others (interdependence). Resolving the layers of pain and bitterness produced by abuse can be gradually accomplished by awareness and communication between the concerned parties, followed by forgiveness. Finally, *healthy* interdependent relationships (such as those of Paul and his colleagues) must be developed to replace the stultifying and nonproductive role playing that often characterizes codependents in a family situation. Interdependence with others in no way precludes that an individual has needs and abilities of his or her own that must be satisfied. A commonly shared goal is best met when all persons involved work toward that goal in ways best suited to their capacities and personality bents.

When codependency is left unchecked, family members are almost always susceptible to holiday depression. When codependency issues are resolved through mutual efforts, holidays can be happier—and so can the rest of the year.

12

Tying Up the Package

A *Los Angeles Daily News* release described the latest and self-described "most unique Christmas musical collection ever." *Bummed Out Christmas* was billed as "an album of anti-Christmas classics that would make Scrooge proud," featuring such "melodic depressants" as "Christmas Eve Can Kill You," "Lonely Christmas Call," "Christmas in Jail," and "Christmas in Vietnam."

When asked why his company would produce such an album, record executive James Austin was quoted as saying, "We're always looking at new ways of approaching Christmas. We realize that for some people the holiday is a bummer."

Such a cynical marketing approach indicates just how widespread holiday unhappiness is. Throughout this book, we have seen some of the factors that contribute to holiday depression. Now it's time to pull things together with some practical suggestions for avoiding the holiday blues and a final biblical perspective on handling depression *whenever* it comes. (Some of this material is intentionally restated, since "repetition" is probably the most important learning principle.)

Practical Steps Toward Happier Holidays

In his prayer in 1 Thessalonians 5:23, the apostle Paul gives us an important spiritual perspective—that man is a unity of "spirit, soul, and body." Thus, problems in one area of life can relate to others. When Paul prays that our "whole [being] . . . be kept blameless until the coming of our Lord Jesus Christ," he provides us with an important clue in how to deal with holiday depression. Spiritual, emotional, and physical factors must all be considered.

Dealing with the Physical Factors

The following guidelines can strengthen us in the physical and medical realm.

1. *Eat wisely.* Including healthful, nourishing foods in your diet will lessen the desire to "top off" with rich holiday desserts. Avoid trays of cookies and other sweets. At parties, opt instead for vegetables with dip or cheese and crackers. Before shopping, decide what sweets are really "necessary" and avoid being swayed by tempting holiday promotional displays. Fruit salad or frozen yogurt can provide an excellent alternative to some of the more traditional calorie-rich holiday foods.

For individuals on strict diets for medical conditions, it is important to ask your doctor how much you can deviate from the regimen for holiday eating. But be careful! A little "cheating" for some individuals—such as diabetics—could cause big problems at inopportune times.

2. *Rest appropriately.* Sleep is frequently the first thing we cut when we need more hours in our day to keep up with the busy holiday routine. Don't do it. Schedule out sleep time if you must, cutting other items from the routine. Avoid late-night baking, gift wrapping, or toy assembly. Tell yourself and others that the household

"closes down" at a certain hour. After that time, no project work is allowed. When you are well rested, you will find yourself more pleasant to be around, better able to enjoy the holidays, and more productive.

3. *Exercise appropriately.* Regular exercise promotes mental health as well as physical well-being. Avoid the lethargy following heavy holiday meals by getting out for a walk, weather permitting. On inclement days take advantage of those large indoor expanses known as shopping malls. Another important physical principle for uncles, dads, and grandpas: Remember that you are not as young as you used to be. When you get together with youngsters at the holidays, resist the urge to attempt to repeat the athletic stunts you performed in college, especially if you have allowed those skills to diminish with the passing of time. Spending time playing with the kids is great, but ending up with pulled muscles, strained backs, or worse is not!

4. *Medical help.* If a medical problem is suspected, don't use the holidays as an excuse for delaying diagnosis and treatment. Doing so not only postpones recovery, but it can ruin a festive occasion for everyone else. When under treatment, follow your doctor's directions. The busy holiday schedule may cause you to alter the amount or frequency of medication or to ignore possible side effects (even one glass of wine can cause problems if combined with certain medications). Be sensitive to your body and communicate with your physician. Take necessary health precautions. The same thing goes for physical therapy. Don't let it slide during the holidays or you may find yourself back at "square one."

5. *Plan and schedule ahead.* In one family, Mom agreed by phone to coordinate the church Christmas program, but Junior came home from school announcing a big part in the holiday program and needing a spe-

cial costume. Sister announced her upcoming participation in the district winter musicale, but Dad announced his intention to host the Christmas office party at home on the same night.

Before such scheduling chaos arises, hold a family conference early enough to discuss the level of commitment that can be expected of each family member and to what activities. Communication and compromise can go a long way toward nipping holiday overcommitment in the bud. Sometimes family members need to get together just to practice politely but firmly using the little word "no."

6. *Avoid overspending.* Protect your financial health by budgeting ahead and shopping early for holiday entertaining and gifts. Watch for sales. Buy throughout the year for such gift-exchange occasions as Christmas or Easter. Utilize special Christmas club accounts at the local bank. Consider giving gifts of time and labor or handmade presents that can be done as individual or family projects. Try to reach a consensus among members of your extended family that gifts for every "special occasion"—birthdays, graduations, anniversaries—are not always necessary. (Some large families have found that it works quite well to draw names, so that each member receives one significant gift rather than several modest or inappropriate ones.)

Avoid credit cards, since these discourage creativity or planning and lead to impulse spending. As one wag put it, "Credit cards roasting on an open fire" provides a wiser alternative than "finance charges nipping at your nose."

Dealing with the Emotional Factors

A second major target area for dealing with holiday depression is the emotional realm.

1. *Recast those idealized past memories with a healthy dose of reality.* You may find it helpful to make a written record of past holidays, including both pros and cons, to avoid inappropriate comparisons that can lead to present depression. Try talking over any past traumas in a healthy context, with a family member, friend, or counselor. Sort out what *really* happened years ago.

2. *Release unfulfilled expectations to God.* This includes both past and present expectations that have led to internalized unresolved emotions. Here again, communicating those emotions to God, to a trusted friend, to the individual involved, and/or to a professional counselor can help prevent depression from occurring. (Go back over the material in chapters 4 and 5, making notes about what applies to your specific situation and what action you need to take as a result.) Remember also to avoid unfulfilled *self*-expectations as well. Don't expect yourself to perform perfectly, give extravagantly, or respond to adversity flawlessly.

We have found it helpful for individuals who are plagued with unfulfilled expectations to sit down with pencil and paper and make a list of everything they have expected and from whom—God, self, and others. When this task is completed, they can symbolically "bundle up" the expectations list, verbalizing in prayer to God that they are giving those unfulfilled expectations to him.

Expect to receive nothing more than what God (and other people) have already given you, telling yourself to view anything extra as a pleasant and positive surprise. Utilize the therapy of thanksgiving. "Count your blessings" by making a list of all God's benefits (Ps. 103:2), remembering that he "daily bears our burdens" (Ps. 68:19). Review this list regularly, particularly when you feel an attack of "If only . . ." coming on.

3. *Resolve to resolve relationships—and do it.* Recently, a nationally syndicated advice columnist received a number of extremely positive letters in response to her suggested "reconciliation day," in which she called on individuals who had experienced long-term alienation from family or friends to move toward peacemaking. It may be helpful to write out precisely what wrong you feel has been done to you. Then list how you would *like* to respond, followed by what you feel would be the most *appropriate* response. Often a pastor or counselor can provide perspective on how to approach reconciliation on the basis of Matthew 18:15–19 and other biblical passages that encourage us to seek to be reconciled with our "brothers."

When attempting reconciliation, it is important to recognize that there is only so much you can do. Paul's instruction: "If it is possible, as far as it depends on you, live at peace with everyone" (Rom. 12:18) implies that some conflicts will not be resolved, no matter how much you want them to be or how hard you try. But give it your best shot ("overcome evil with good" [v. 21]), and then leave the rest to God.

It is also important to forgive yourself for not being perfect and for past wrongs you may have done. A high degree of depression, holiday and otherwise, is directly related to grudges against ourselves (depression is anger turned inward). First make sure that you are not holding yourself to an unrealistically high standard. Then recognize that since Christ can forgive you, you can both forgive yourself and experience the forgiveness of others. Bitterness has been described as self-cannibalism, and the ultimate answer to bitterness is to forgive as Christ has forgiven us (Eph. 4:32).

4. *Learn to balance your obsessive-compulsive, perfectionist personality.* Frequently, holidays are times when

these personality traits are intensified. Seek and listen to feedback from others regarding how much you are doing and why. Ask yourself if you are using work, personal busyness, or community activities to avoid intimate relationships. Remember two important practical antidotes to being overly committed to a schedule of "must do" assignments—priorities and balance!

5. *Deal with loneliness.* Watch yourself for the tendency to withdraw from people, especially when troubled. Develop a specific and reasonable plan for spending time with spouse, family, and close friends. Don't force yourself to spend a large amount of time with people you don't enjoy, but be sure to seek the opportunity for interaction with those with whom you can be yourself and have fun. One important strategy for overcoming loneliness that already exists is to develop the heart of a servant. Look for opportunities to be of help to others, and this will focus your attention on them rather than on yourself (see chapter 7).

6. *Process your grief.* Recognize the presence and extent of pain from past holiday-related losses. Share feelings about these. Work through the steps of grief to resolution, either personally or, better yet, with a friend or counselor. Learn to get emotions out in the open. Learn to cry as well as laugh. It may be painful to examine those emotions, but the alternative of leaving them buried is almost sure to lead to depression.

Dealing with the Spiritual Factors

The third major area for coping with holiday depression involves your spiritual life.

1. *Focus on the spiritual significance of the holidays.* Review the material in chapter 2 as you prepare for specific holidays, asking yourself: "What is the specific purpose for this particular holiday?" *and* "How can my

family and I best implement that purpose in our lives?"
Answering those questions will help you follow the next
two suggestions.

2. *Make holidays a time of personal spiritual growth.*
Holidays can either hinder or help you spiritually. Carve
out special times for personal devotions and family worship. Despite a busy schedule, seek to give more rather
than less time to reading and meditating on Scripture.
Focus on great hymns that are geared to specific holidays and are rich in theology. Memorize pertinent
Scripture verses and establish the tradition of sharing
them with loved ones.

3. *Review past holiday blessings.* Perhaps God has
worked in a significant way to meet your needs. Share
your thankfulness, too, with family and friends. Make
every holiday an occasion for acknowledging God's benefits and recounting them to others, as you encourage
them to do the same.

4. *Avoid sin scrupulously.* Holidays can be times when
you are particularly susceptible to temptation. Be wary!
Take precautions to avoid "the path of the wicked" (Prov.
4:14). Paul reminds us of both the practical danger and
positive alternative to gratifying "the desires of the sinful
nature" (Rom. 13:14).

If you do backslide, it is important to confess your sin
to God (1 John 1:9), to confess to others when appropriate (James 5:16), to accept and acknowledge God's forgiveness, and then to forgive yourself and move on.

5. *Trusting Christ as Savior.* The ultimate key to overcoming holiday depression involves a personal relationship with Christ, based on his promised provision of all
our needs, including forgiveness for our sins. If you have
not yet trusted Christ as your personal Savior, why not
do so now? If you have, renew your commitment and
look for holiday occasions to share the reality of faith in

Christ with others. Invite them to trust the One who is the ultimate source of love, joy, and peace.

Biblical Perspectives on Depression

Perhaps you have read this far and are still struggling with depression, holiday or otherwise. You may even understand some of the reasons you are so downcast and have tried most or all of the practical steps—and still have experienced little or no relief. The following vignette from the life of Jesus Christ, God's perfect Son, may just be the perspective you need to deal with your depression. After all, if a person as perfect as Jesus Christ could feel depressed and take steps to overcome those feelings, perhaps we can benefit from examining and applying the approach he took.

The occasion was the night before his crucifixion. The emotions he expressed, as described in Matthew 26:37–38, provide indisputable evidence that Jesus did feel depressed about the fate he knew awaited him—he was "overwhelmed with sorrow." Clearly, then, depression is not always a direct result of personal sin or a reaction to past events or "imaginary" future troubles.

Although recognizing that *you* are imperfect, seek to identify with Christ at this dark point in his earthly life. Omniscient, he knows not only the fact of what he is already facing but also the reality and extent of the suffering he will shortly endure. He is aware of the faltering hearts of his closest associates and is able to anticipate their impending defection and denial. Most of all, he senses a coming separation never before experienced—an alienation between himself and his perfect Father. Their previously unbroken and eternal fellowship will be fractured at the point at which Christ becomes a sin offering to provide redemption for humankind.

Facing this situation, the Savior took three significant

steps to alleviate his feelings of depression—steps we can also apply.

First, *he utilized the resources of good friends,* his closest earthly associates. Knowing what lay ahead and feeling sorrow within his soul, Jesus reached out to Peter, James, and John. He called on them to go with him to Gethsemane, then communicated his feelings to them candidly. He explained, "The sorrow in my heart is so great that it almost crushes me. Stay here and keep watch with me" (Matt. 26:38, TEV).

Shortly thereafter, these beloved disciples, who were apparently weary, dozed off (v. 40). Yet when our Lord found them asleep, he didn't give up on them or withdraw from their presence. In fact, even though they had let him down, he continued to accept and even encourage them to "pray so that you will not fall into temptation" (v. 42).

Sometimes when we feel depressed, we have a tendency to exaggerate the importance of others' failures and reject them as a result. We must not allow the shortcomings of others to cause us to withdraw, thereby missing an opportunity to utilize the resources and fellowship of family, close friends, or other people who might be supportive.

The second step the Savior took to deal with his feelings of depression was to *express his feelings to God in prayer* (v. 39). The conversation between Christ and his Father recorded by Matthew presupposes the presence of an intimate relationship between Father and Son. Today, many people who attempt prayer when depressed eventually come to say, "This just doesn't work." If this has been your experience, perhaps you need to ask yourself candidly, "Do I have a personal relationship with God? Have I genuinely trusted Christ as Savior so that I am in a position where he can answer me through his

Holy Spirit? Am I allowing God to answer my prayers through his Word and through circumstances of his own choosing, rather than simply insisting on what I personally want or how I think the situation should be worked out?"

It is refreshing to note the absence of pious platitudes or bargaining pleas in the cry of Christ: "My Father, if it is possible, may this cup be taken from me. Yet not as I will, but as you will" (Matt. 26:39). Christ was in *complete* submission to the will of the Father, which should be our attitude, too, in any prayer request. Jesus simply voices his honest feelings to his Father. We are privileged to do the same. Although God knows our thoughts already, he has invited us to communicate honestly with him "so that we may receive mercy and find grace to help us in our time of need" (Heb. 4:16).

After candidly voicing his feelings, Christ chose to accept the experiences the Father was permitting in his life, and to trust him to accomplish what was best. When this ingredient of complete trust is missing from our lives, increased feelings of depression and despair often follow.

Persistence in expressing our feelings to God in prayer and in meditating on God's promises can help us develop the kind of confident faith capable of withstanding the storms and adversities of life. Frequently our feelings of depression and despair will begin to dissipate as we, like Christ in Gethsemane, persist in prayer, verbalize our feelings honestly to God, then trust him to graciously work out the details of our dilemma.

The third step in our Savior's response to depression followed quite naturally from the second. At this point Jesus *took action to face squarely the source of his feelings of depression.* He could have succumbed to the temptation to flee the scene of his betrayal and ultimate arrest. Instead, Jesus submitted to the impending crisis, trusting his Father for its outcome. Such action is rarely easy, but when we delay dealing with conflicts, losses, or other factors that may trigger depression, we increase our feelings of anguish and hopelessness.

At times your feelings of depression may be mild and short-lived. On other occasions they may be so severe that you are kept from functioning normally. (Never delay seeking counsel for yourself or a loved one whenever depression or other psychological dysfunction prevents participation in the basic activities of daily living or leads to suicidal feelings.) If your feelings of depression are not severe and persistent enough to require professional help, you may be able to implement the three steps taken by Christ in Gethsemane. Whether facing holiday depression, a grief reaction, or depression triggered by some other circumstance, you can utilize the resources of good friends and family (including your mate) who genuinely care for you; *and* you can express yourself candidly and trustingly to God in prayer; *and* you can initiate action to face and deal with the source of your depression. Implementing these steps can lead to happier holidays—and to depression-free daily living throughout the year.